Crochet

- made easy

Crochet

- made easy

Anne-Lise Hald

Akacia

Anne-Lise Hald (born 1965) graduated from „Hellerup Håndarbejds-seminarium". She owns her own company which sells crafts designs. She produces crocheting and knitting handwork for several Danish magazines.

© 2004 Anne-Lise Hald and
Forlaget Akacia
Skovvænget 1
5690 Tommerup
Denmark
email: akacia@akacia.dk

Text, models and drawings: Anne-Lise Hald
Translation: Forlaget Akacia
Photos: Black/White - Anne-Lise & Rene Hald
        Colour - Poul Erik Nikolajsen
DTP: Forlaget Akacia

Printed at Øko-Tryk I/S, Videbæk, Denmark, 2004

ISBN: 87-7847-058-7

Contents

Introduction

I had my debut in crocheting when I was 7 years old. I was so lucky that my maternal and paternal grandmother both had a large knowledge within handwork. Their patience was also very large, which was much needed when I got myself tangled up in a bungle of yarn and was waving a crochet needle wildly around in the air while practising the different stitches.

When I had first learned how to make the stitches I crocheted like crazy. I produced a large number of funny and unique animals, caps, scarves, dolls clothes and bags. So in a way you might say that nothing much has changed because this is what I still do. My old crocheted animals have become a part of my childrens favorite toys.

Today, being a trained handwork teacher, I am still crazy about crocheting. I have always had a weakness for crocheted objects and when my grandmother's crochet work was given to me, it was the beginning of a still growing collection of crochet works from 1880 to the present.

In this book I have been inspired by older patterns, which have been used for modern designs for which diagrammes have been made. There are many levels of difficulty in this book so theres is something for the beginner as well as the more experienced in the fine art of crocheting.. DMC yarn has been used for the designs in this book.

Enjoy!

Privatly owned. Crocheted horse. Measures about 30 x 30 cm. My first crocheted horse was created in the summer of 1973. It is crocheted in brown acrylic yarn made with double crochets..

My grandmothers old pattern book with crochet tests - a very good source of inspiration.

How to crochet

Position of the hand: Hold the crochet hook as a pencil. Then put the hook into the loop, while your left hand thumb and middle finger hold the work. Put the thread over your index finger like in knitting.

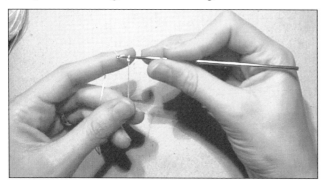

Tip: when crocheting with smooth thread or if you crochet very loosely, it may often be a help to wrap the thread around your little finger before taking it over your index finger.

A row of chain stitches is called a chain and is used for among other things making a starting chain and turning chain. When counting stitches in a chain always count from the first loop and towards the crochet hook. The loop on the crochet hook is never counted.

Turning chain: At the end of a row you always make a number of chain stitches before turning the work. These chain stitches are called a turning chain and gives height to the next row and makes the edges even. The amount of chain stitches needed depends on which stitches you are making. The turning chain replaces the first stitch in the next row.

The amount of turning stitches are as follows:
Slip stitch: 1 chain stitch
Double crochet: 1 chain stitch
Half treble: 2 chain stitches
Treble: 3 chain stitches
Double treble: 4 chain stitches
Triple treble: 5 chain stitches
Quadruple treble: 6 chain stitches

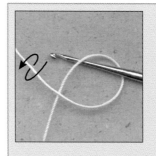

How to make a starting chain: Make a loop as shown on the photo. Put the crochet hook into the loop.......

........carefully pull until the loop fits around the hook. Thus is the first stitch made.

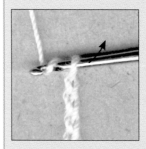

Chain stitch: ch

Take the hook under the thread over your left index finger - this is called thread or yarn over - and pull the thread through the chain with the hook= 1 chain. Continue until you have as many chain as you need.

× Double crochet: dc

Make a length of chain, insert the hook from the front under the two top threads of the 2nd chain from the hook, thread over and draw it through the chain. There are now 2 loops on the hook. Thread over again and draw through the 2 loops = 1 double crochet.

8

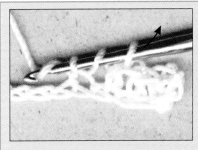

 Half treble: htr

Make a length of chain. Thread over, insert the hook from the front under the two top threads of the 3rd chain from the hook, thread over and draw it through the chain. Thread over again and draw it through all three loops = 1 half treble.

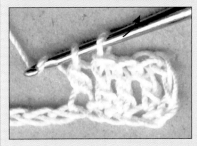

 Treble = tr

Make a length of chain. Thread over and insert the hook from the front under the two top threads of the 4th chain from the hook, thread over and draw the thread through the stitch. There are now 3 loops on the hook. Thread over , draw the thread through the first two loops, thread over again and draw through the remaining 2 loops on the hook = 1 treble.

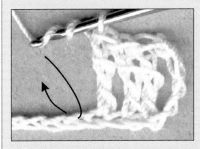

 Double treble: dtr

Make a length of chain, thread over twice, insert the hook from the front under the two top threads of the 5th chain from the hook. Thread over and draw it through the chain, thread over and draw through the first two loops on the hook. There are now 3 loops on the hook. Thread over again and draw the thread through the next 2 loops on the hook. There are now 2 loops left, thread over again and draw through the remaining 2 loops = 1 double treble.

Triple treble: ttr

Thread over three times, insert the hook from the front in the 6th chain from the hook, thread over and draw the thread through chain, (thread over and draw through 2 loops on the hook) 4 times = triple treble.

Qaudruple treble: quadtr

Thread over four times, insert needle in chain,

thread over and draw the thread through the chain, (thread over and draw through 2 loops on the hook) 5 times = quadruple treble.

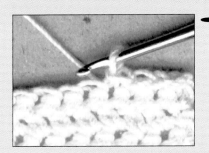

 Slip stitch: sl st

Here the slip stitch is shown with double crochet. Insert the hook from the front under the 2 top threads of the stitch next to the hook, thread over and draw it through the stitch and the loop on the hook in one movement = 1 slip stitch. The slip stitch is "an invisible stitch" since it does not create much depth. Used for joining a round in circular crocheting or when decreasing.

Loop of stitches From the 2nd row you always pick up the two top threads of each stitch unlees otherwise stated.

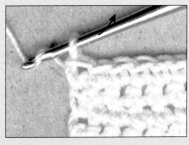

To finish off When the last chain is made, make an extra chain stitch, then break the thread and draw it through the last remaining loop. This way you lock the last stitch. Weave the thread into the back of the work.

Decreasing

By 1 stitch: Crochet 2 double crochets together like this: Insert the hook through the first stitch, thread over and draw the thread through the stitch, there are now 2 loops on the hook. Insert the hook through the next stitch, thread over and draw through it = 3 loops on the hook. Thread over and draw the thread through all 3 loops at the same time = 1 stitch.

Decreasing of more stitches at the beginning of the row: Make slip stitches over the stitches which are decreased. At the end of the row you do not crochet the stitches.

Increasing

By 1(2) stitch(es): When using double crochet, treble and so on, increase with 1(2) stitch(es) by crocheting into the same stitch 2(3) times.

Tips for left-handed crocheting:
It is easy to invert the photos. A quick solution is a hand mirror held to the photo. The reflected image now shows the left-hand version.
A more permanent solution is to make a copy of the photos on an overhead transparent. Turn the backside up and it is ready for use.
Overhead folie may be purchased in stationary shops and it may be used in the copying machine just like common paper.

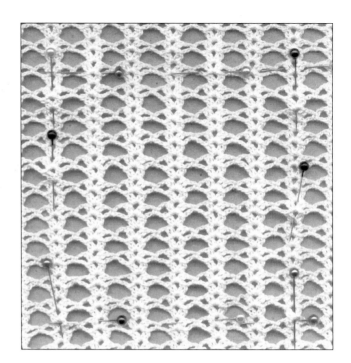

Tension

When crocheting a crochet pattern there is always stated a tension, which must be kept if the work is to maintain the measurement. Therefore it is a good idea always to make a test swatch to be sure that the tension is correct before starting the actual work.

This is done in the following way: make a few more stitches on the starting chain than is stated in the tension of the crochet pattern, making the test a bit larger than 10x10 cm (perhaps 11 cm). Then lay the test swatch flat on a table and with pins mark the measurements, which are given in the crochet pattern. Carefully count the rows and stitches between the pins.

If there are too many stitches, try with a thinner hook. If there are too few stitches, try using a thicker hook, until your own tension matches the one given in the pattern. It may seem a bit tedious to make such a test swatch, but in the end it may be worthwhile because the amount of stitches, and consequently the measurements of the work, given in the pattern may never fit.

Washing instructions

It is a pity if a work is ruined due to washing it incorrectly. Usually it is stated on the band of the yarn how the said yarn must be washed. Crochet works should be washed by hand. Never wash it in a washing machine because the stitches may be lose shape.

Large plaids, bedspreads and curtains just have to be thoroughly steamed through without the iron touching the work itself, thus avoiding squashing the stitches and losing their volume.

Slow drying, meaning stretched out with pins and covered with a moist piece of fabric, ensures that your crochet work maintains its shape.

Stretching

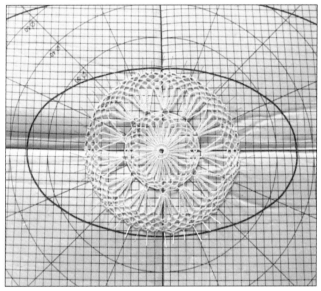

When washing smaller items like for example doilies, insertions and laces it may be an advantage to stretch the work out while it is still wet, to keep it completely even and smooth.

Stretch out the work so the measurements matches the one given in the pattern. Put rustless pins in every row or bow, the more pins the better. All details and edges are straightened out with pins, which remain in the work until it is dry.

Stretching board

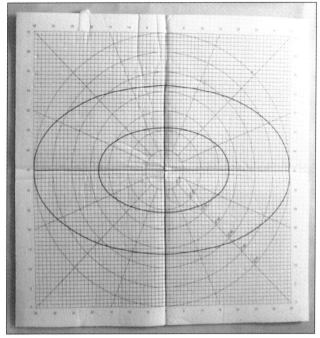

A good remedy is a stretching board. The board is consists of foam rubber covered with fabric, which is easy to put pins in. The surface has printed circles and oval shapes and cm specifications to make it easier to stretch the work. After use the mat can be folded so it will not take up so much space.

Starching

Starching of smaller crocheted works. Doilies are very good when you want to protect the furniture. Once in a while they have to be washed and then it may be difficult to make them presentable again. In the following there is described an easy way to starch doilies and other crocheted work.

I use one leaf of gelatine for each doily. Soak the gelatine leaf in cold water for about 5 minutes. Take the gelatine out of the water without pressing the water out. After this put it in a bowl over a pot with simmering water and melt the gelatine leaf. Cool the liquid a bit. Dip the newly washed doily in the liquid and squeeze any surplus water out of the doily. Stretch the doily with rustless pins. Let it dry stretched out.

After a drying time of about 24 hours the doily is completely dry and ready to use.

Abbreviations

beg:	beginning
d:	double
dtr:	double treble
dc:	double crochet
g:	gramme
rep:	repeat
gr(s):	group(s)
htr(s):	half treble(s)
dec:	decrease
sl st(s):	slip stitch(es)
ch(s):	chain(s)
st(s):	stitch(es)
rnd(s):	round(s)
row(s):	row(s)
yoh:	yarn over hook
tog:	together
cl:	cluster
tr:	treble
inc:	increase
dtr cross st:	double treble cross stitch

Chart symbols

▷	Start here
▶	End here
⬯	Chain
▬	Slip stitch
×	Double crochet
Ꞁ	Half treble
Ƒ	Treble
Ⅎ	Double treble
∓	Triple treble
∓	Quadruple treble
⋏	A 2 treble cluster over 2 stitches
⋔	A 3 treble cluster over 3 stitches
⋔	A 3 double treble cluster over 3 stitches
⋔	A 4 double treble cluster over 4 stitches
⋔	A 3 triple treble cluster worked over 3 stitches
⋌	A 2 triple treble cluster worked over 2 stitches
⅄	3 double crochet worked into one stitch

⬯	Long loop
⬭	A 4 half treble cluster worked into one stitch
⬭	A 3 treble cluster worked into one stitch
⬭	A 4 treble cluster worked into one stitch
⬭	A 2 double treble cluster worked into one stitch
⬭	A 3 double treble cluster worked into one stitch
⬭	A 2 triple treble cluster worked into one stitch
⬭	A 2 triple treble cluster worked into one stitch
⬭	A 3 triple treble cluster worked into one stitch
⬭	A 3 triple treble cluster worked into one stitch
⬭	A 4 triple treble cluster worked into one stitch
⋈	Double treble cross stitch
▬▬▬	5 chain

Borders & Corners

Borders

Five different borders are illustrated in this section. The borders are crocheted on unbleached linen with twelve threads per cm. White Babylo no. 20/12 from DMC is used. Running length approx 400 meters/50 g. Crochet needle no. 1.25.

Preparing the fabric: Cut out the fabric to the required size. Zigzag the edges in order to prevent fraying. Fold in the edges approx 1 cm and iron the edges until they are sharp.

Chain border

This is a very charming and simple border. It looks great on a t-shirt or as edging on a blouse. You could for example make it in a contrasting colour.

Diagram for chain border.

Follow the diagram

Take the needle through the fabric approx three to four threads below the edge of the fabric and work 1 ch, *5 ch, miss ten to twelve threads, 1 dc three to four threads below the edge of the fabric, rep from * to complete the rnd, finish with 1 sl st worked in the first ch.

Break the thread and fasten off.

> **Tips.** The borders are suitable on for example handkerchiefs. It is possible to buy handkerchiefs that come with hemstitches that are ready to use, so you do not have to prepare the fabric yourself.

Double crochet border with picots

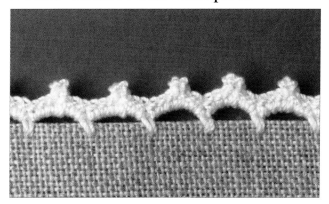

A striking and very simple border that looks like a row of buttonhole loops lying along the edge of the fabric.

Diagram for double crochet border with picots.
The border is made in two rnds.

Follow the diagram

Rnd 1: Fasten the thread 3-4 threads below the edge of the fabric with 1 ch, *5 ch, miss 10 to 12 threads, 1 dc into the edge, rep from *, finish with 1 sl st in the first ch of the rnd.

Rnd 2: 1 ch = 1 dc, 2 dc in the ch * 1 picot = 3 ch, 1 sl st in the first ch, 3 dc, 3 dc in ch, rep from *, finish with 1 sl st in the first ch of the rnd.

Break the thread and fasten off.

Ruffled border

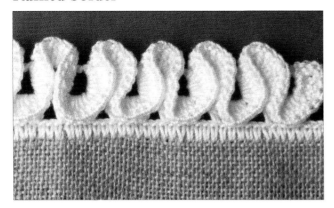

This very cute three-dimensional border gives an exciting effect.

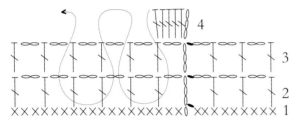

Diagram for ruffled border. The border is worked in 4 rounds. Crochet the ruffle in the direction the arrow points.

Follow the diagram.

Rnd 1: Fasten the thread at the edge of the fabric with 1 ch, continue to work dc 3-4 threads below the edge the rest of the rnd, finish the rnd with 1 sl st in the first ch of the rnd.

Rnd 2 + 3: 5 ch, * miss 2 st, 1 tr in the next st, 2 ch, rep from *, finish with 1 sl st in the 3rd ch of the rnd.

Rnd 4: 3 ch, 5 tr over 2 ch, *6 tr rnd the tr from the first rnd, 6 tr over 2 ch from rnd 2, 6 tr over the tr from the first rnd, 6 tr over 2 ch, rep from * following the arrow. Finish the rnd with 1 sl st in the 3rd ch from the beg of the rnd.

Airy lace border

This airy lace border is a beautiful conclusion on smaller items as for example handkerchiefs.

Diagram for airy lace border made in 3 rounds.

Follow the diagram.

Round 1: Fasten the thread at the edge of the fabric with 1 ch, continue to work sl st on the edge approx 3-4 threads below for the rest of the rnd, conclude the rnd with a sl st.

Round 2: 6 ch, * miss 3 st, 3 dc over 3 dc, 5 ch, rep from *, finish with 1 sl st in the first ch.

Round 3: 2 sl st over 2 ch, 1 ch, *3 ch, 1 dc into the same arc, 5 ch, in the next ch 1 dc, rep from *, finish with 1 sl st in the first ch of the rnd.

	Ch: chain		**Tr:** treble
	Sl st: slip stitch		**Start:** Start here
×	**Dc:** double crochet		**End:** End here

Corners

Materials: Approx 50 g white Babylo no. 20/12 from DMC. Running length approx 400 metres/50 g. Crochet hook no. 1.25. Unbleached linen with 12 threads per cm.

Preparing the fabric: Cut out the fabric to the required size. Zigzag the edges of the fabric in order to prevent fraying. Fold in the edges approx one cm and iron the edges until they are sharp.

Scallop border with picots

This decorative scallop border with picots is quick to make. The space between the scallops may be varied.

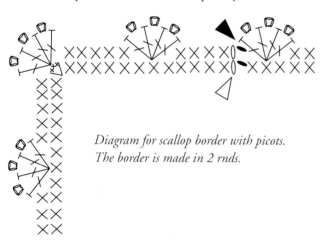

Diagram for scallop border with picots. The border is made in 2 rnds.

Round 1: Follow the diagram. Fasten the thread at the edge of the fabric with 1 ch, work dc the rest of the rnd, finish with 1 sl st in the first ch.

Rnd 2: 1 ch, 4 dc over 4 dc, miss 1 dc, make *(1 tr, 1 picot = 3 ch, 1 sl st in the first ch) in the next st 3 times + 1 tr, miss 1 dc, 5 tr over 5 tr, rep from *, finish with 1 sl st in the first ch of the rnd.

Pointed border

The pointed border makes a beautiful frame around the fabric squares.

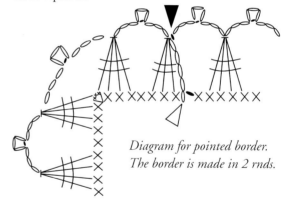

Diagram for pointed border. The border is made in 2 rnds.

Rnd 1: Follow the diagram. Fasten the thread at the edge of the fabric with 1 ch, work dc the rest of the rnd, finish with 1 sl st in the first ch.

Rnd 2: 4 ch, work a 3 dtr cl over the next 3 st, *3 ch, 1 picot = 3 ch + sl st in the first ch, 3 ch, miss 1 ch, work a 4 d tr cl over the next 4 st, rep from *, finish with 1 sl st in the 4th ch of the rnd.

> **Tips about corners:**
> You can for example use a mirror when you make a corner. In this way it is possible to see how the corner may look when it is finished.

Scallop border

A close scallop border with a single picot.

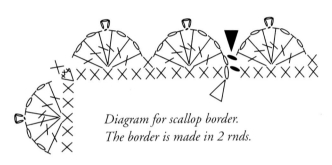

Diagram for scallop border. The border is made in 2 rnds.

Rnd 1: Follow the diagram, Fasten the thread at the edge of the fabric with 1 ch, crochet dc for the first rnd, finish off with 1 sl st in the 1st ch.

Rnd 2: 1 ch, *miss 2 dc, crochet in the next st (1 tr + 1 ch) twice + 1 tr + 1 picot = 3 ch + 1 sl st in the 1st ch + (1 tr + 1 ch) twice + 1 tr, miss 2 dc, 1 dc in the next dc, rep from * the rest of the rnd, finish with 1 sl st in the 1st ch of the rnd.

Flower border

A beautiful flower border frames this doily. But you can use this border on many other things.

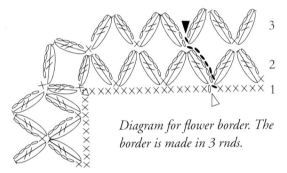

Diagram for flower border. The border is made in 3 rnds.

Rnd 1: Follow the diagram. Fasten the thread at the edge of the fabric with 1 ch, make dc the rest of the rnd, finish with 1 sl st in the 1st ch.

Rnd 2: 5 ch, a 2 d tr cl worked in one ch, *miss 5 dc, work a 2 d tr cl + 4 ch + 1 dc + 4 ch + 2 dtr cl, rep from * to * the rest of the rnd, finish the rnd with 1 sl st in the 1st ch of the rnd. Work 5 sl st over 5 st.

Rnd 3: 5 ch, 2 dtr cl in 1 ch, *work 2 dtr cl at the top of the next 2 dtr cl + 4 ch + 1 sl st + 4 ch + 2 dtr cl, rep from * the rest of the rnd, finish off with 1 sl st in the 1st ch of the rnd.

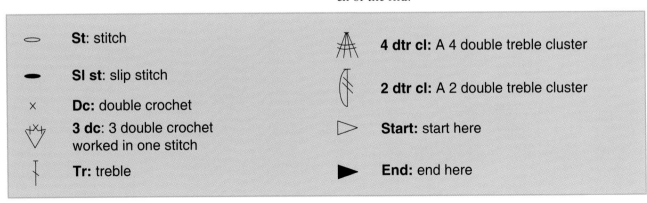

⬯	**St**: stitch	🗚	**4 dtr cl**: A 4 double treble cluster
⬮	**Sl st**: slip stitch	∮	**2 dtr cl**: A 2 double treble cluster
×	**Dc**: double crochet	▷	**Start**: start here
⋎	**3 dc**: 3 double crochet worked in one stitch	►	**End**: end here
⊤	**Tr**: treble		

Yards and yards of lace

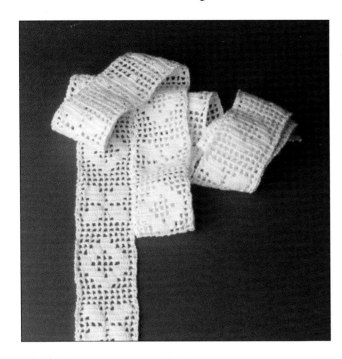

Materials: Approx 20 g white Cordonnet Special no. 20 from DMC. Running length 160 m/20 g. Crochet hook no. 1.25.

Dimensions: The width of the lace is approx 4,5 cm.

Lace: Work 33 ch. Follow the diagram.

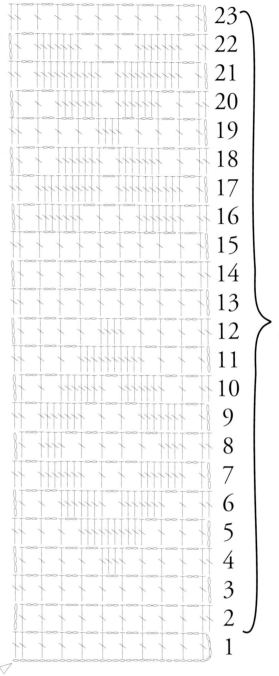

Diagram for filet crochet. Row 2 – 23 features the pattern and is repeated throughout the work.

How to make filet crochet

If you have never tried to make filet crochet before, then have a look at these detailed photos that show you how to make filet crochet.

1. Here the signature and the photo for an open mesh are shown. An open mesh consists of 1 treble worked in the treble from the previous round, 2 chain, miss 2 stitches, 1 treble in the treble from the previous round.

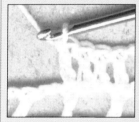

2. A filled mesh consists of 4 treble which are worked over 4 stitches from the previous round, please notice that the 2 treble are worked around the 2 chain from the previous round. If you work over a filled mesh from the previous round, then you would have to work 4 trebles over the 4 trebles from the previous round.

Here you can see 3 rounds with filled and empty meshes.

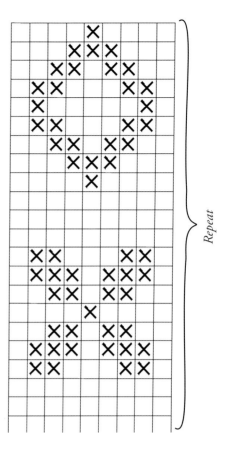

Repeat

Chart symbols for filet crochet

□ = 2 chain, miss 2 stitches, 1 treble in the next stitch.

✕ = 4 trebles

✕|✕ = 7 trebles

✕|✕|✕ = 10 trebles. This means that for every additional cross, you work 3 more treble.

Please remember that all rounds start with 3 chains replacing the first treble of the round.

Tips about making your own pattern

It is easy to make your own pattern for filet crochet on chequered paper by making a pattern of crosses. You may also be inspired by cross-stitch patterns, which may easily be translated into filet crochet. The pattern from the opposite side is also shown here where it is drawn in this way.

Hardanger insertion

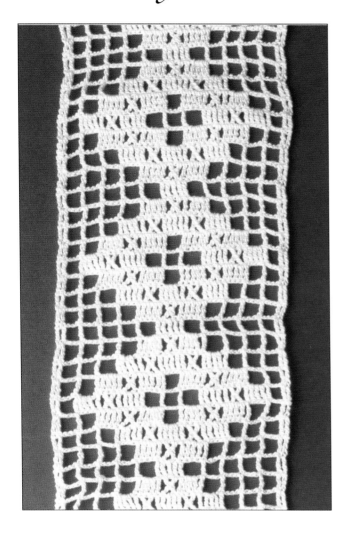

A very beautiful insertion highly inspired by Hardanger. It is really a variation of filet crochet where the pattern consists of a combination of double treble and double treble cross stitches.

The lace is worked across for yards and yards, which is very convenient if you have not quite decided what to use it for.

Materials: Approx 50 g white Babylo no. 20/12 from DMC. Running length approx 400 m/50 g. Crochet hook no. 1.50.

⌒	**Ch:** chain
⫡	**Dtr:** double treble
⤬	**Dtr cross:** double treble cross
▷	**Start:** Start here

How to make a crossed double treble

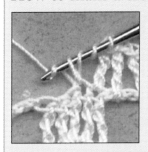 Yarn over the hook twice, take the hook through the next stitch, yarn over the hook and pull the yarn through the stitch = 4 loops on the hook…

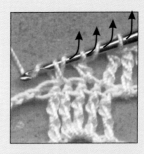 … yarn over and pull through the stitch = 5 loops on the hook. (Yarn over, pull through the 2 first loops on the hook) 4 times.

 …yarn over and pull through the 2 first loops on the hook = 3 loops on the hook.

 Make 1 chain and 1 treble at the crossing through both chain loops..

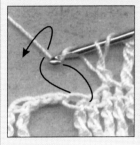 Yarn over, miss 1 stitch and put the hook through the next stitch…

 … = 1 crossed double treble.

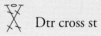 Dtr cross st

Diagram for Hardanger insertion.
2nd – 9th row makes out the pattern and is repeated until the work is as long as you want it to be.

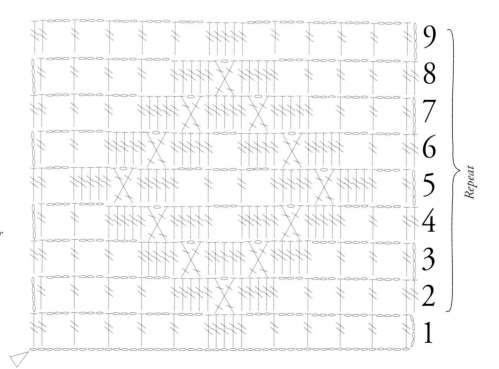

Mesh insertion

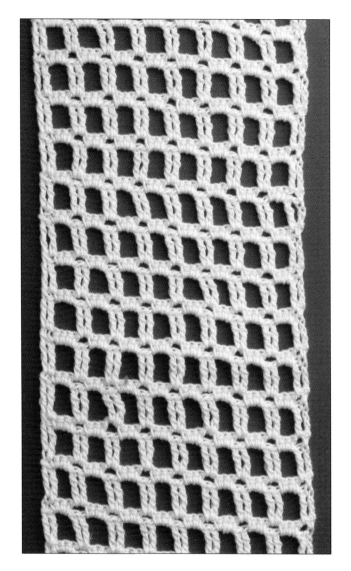

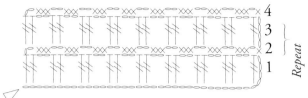

Diagram for mesh insertion. The 2nd and 3rd rows make the pattern and they are repeated until the work obtains the desired length.

Pretty insertion worked in a combined pattern inspired by filet crochet, made from double treble and double crochet. The pattern is very simple and easy and it is very suitable for larger areas.

Materials: Approx 50 g white Babylo no. 20/12 from DMC. Running length approx 400 m/50 g. Hook no. 1,50.

Dimension: The width of the lace is approx 7,5 cm.

Tension: 26 st x 11 rows = 5 x 5 cm.

Insertion: work 37 ch. Follow the diagram.

Tips

The mesh may be worked in any width; you just have to pay attention to the fact that the pattern must be divided with 4 + 5 chain. An example of how many stitches to start out with could be 52 chains, which can be divided with 4 + 1 chain + 4 turning chains. This means that you have to make 57 chains to make the pattern add up.

⌒	**Ch:**	chain
×	**Dc:**	double crochet
‡	**Dtr:**	double treble
▷	**Start:**	Start here

Crocheted trimming

Materials: approx 50 g white Babylo no. 20 from DMC. Running length approx 400 m/50 g. Crochet hook no. 1.5.

Dimensions: Width approx 3 cm.

2(3) triple treble cluster: ((Yarn over the hook 3 times, insert the hook in the stitch, yarn over the hook and pull through the stitch, (yarn over the hook and pull through 2 loops) 3 times)) 2(3) times all in all, yarn over the hook and pull through the remaining 3(4) loops = 2(3) triple treble cluster.

Trimming

Follow the diagram and photo at the same time. Work 10 ch. Form a ring with 1 sl st in the 1st ch. *5 ch, 2 ttr cl worked in the ring…

… 3 ch, 3 ttr cl worked in the ring, 3 ch. 3 ttr cl, 10 ch, 1 sl st in the ring, turn the work…

… 1 ch, work 3 dc around the 10 ch (1 picot = 3 ch, 1 sl st in last dc, 4 dc) 3 times…

… 4 dc in the next ch ring, 6 ch, miss 3 ch, 4 dc over the ch ring, 10 ch, 1 sl st in the ch ring, turn the work…

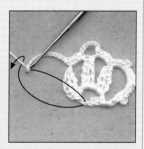

… 1 ch, work 3 dc around the 10 ch (1 picot, 4 dc) 3 times, 4 sl st over the first 4 dc + 2 sl st over 2 ch*.

Now you have completed the first flower, repeat from * to * until the trimming is the desired length. Break the thread and fasten off.

Repeat

Diagram for trimming. The arrows and the numbers show in which direction to work. Start at the starting arrow and then follow the direction of the arrow in numerical order. Repeat the parenthesis until the trimming reaches the required length.

Tips

This is a very pretty trimming that may be used many places around the house, for example as a beautiful curtain string. Trimmings are really a kind of decorative ribbon that is mainly made by hand just like passementerie. It is especially used for furnishing textiles.

⬭	**Ch:** chain
⬬	**Sl st:** slip stitch
×	**Dc:** double crochet
⬭	**3 cl dtr:** 3 double treble cluster worked into one stitch
▷	**Start:** Start here

Lace with fan pattern

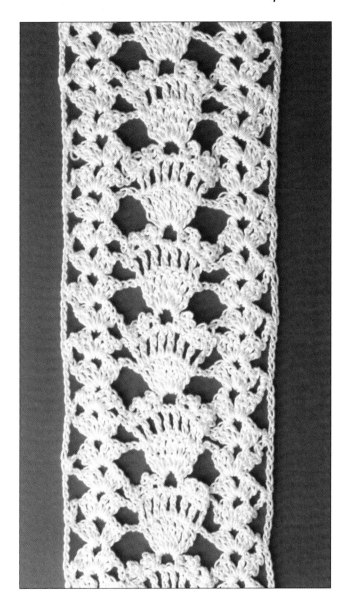

It is always interesting to crochet lace. This very beautiful fan lace may be made in whatever length is required. The pattern is easily learned, you decide the length.

Dimension: Approx 6 cm wide.

Materials: Approx 50 g white Babylo no. 20/12 from DMC. Running length approx 400 m/50 g. Crochet hook 1.25.

Please notice that the parenthesis is repeated the number of times stated right after.

Fan lace

Make 27 chains. Follow the diagram.
Row 3 – 5 make the pattern, rep until the work obtains the required length.

Finish off with working a border along the sides. Fasten the thread off in the first ch ring with 1 sl st, *5 ch and 1 dc in the next ch ring, rep from * over all ch rings in the opposite side.
Break the thread. Fasten off in the opposite side in the same way and make another similar edge.

Tip – This is the easiest way to follow a diagram.
To form a general view of where you are in a crochet diagram, mark the round you are working at like this. Place a pencil 1 round over the round you are about to make. Thus the pattern and the round/row you are about to start at visible.

⌒	**Ch:** chain
▬	**Sl st:** slip stitch
×	**Dc:** double crochet
⊺	**Tr:** treble
∓	**Dtr:** double treble
▷	**Start:** Start here

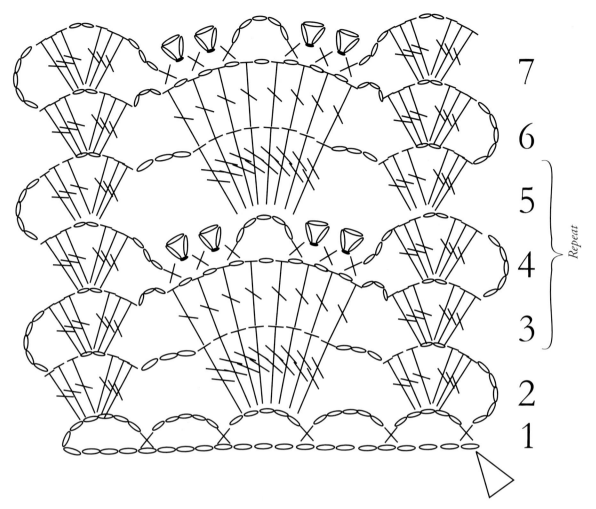

7

6

5

4 Repeat

3

2

1

Diagram for lace with fan pattern. The parenthesis is repeated until the lace has the required length.

Crochet backpack

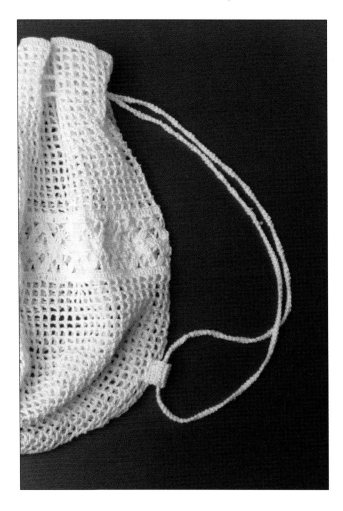

This cute, summery backpack is made in filet crochet with an inserted lace that breaks the pattern.

Dimension: diameter approx 20 cm and height 26 cm.

Materials: Approx 50 g white Cebelia no. 20 from DMC. Running length approx 380 m/50 g. Crochet hook 1.25.

Tension: 10 x 10 meshes = 5 cm.

Crochet backpack: Work 6 ch, 1 sl st in the first ch.

Follow the diagram.
Work inc after the diagram until rnd 18. This means that the inc in rnd 5 – 6 is made over the same place. Work 7 inc = 108 meshes, after which you work straight up until you have completed 30 rnds.

Rnd 31: 3 ch, continue with 1 tr over every st the rest of the rnd = 324 tr.

Rnd 32: Follow along in the diagram at the same time. 1 ch = the 1st dc of the round *3 ch, miss 2 tr, work 1 leaf in the next st/3 dtr + 7 ch + 1 leaf/3 dtr, 3 ch, miss 2 tr, 1 dc in the next st. Rep from * and finish the rnd with 1 sl st, work 7 sl over 7 ch.

Rnd 33: 1 ch = the first dc of the rnd, *4 ch, 1 leaf/2 dtr in the first ch, but without completing the leaf = 3 loops on the hook. Miss 3 ch, work a new leaf/3 dtr, without finishing = 6 loops on the hook, miss 7 st and work another leaf/3 dtr. Yo and pull the thread through all 9 loops on the hook, work 4 ch, then leaf/2 dtr in the joining st from the 9 dtr, miss 3 st, 1 dc in the next ch. Rep from * and finish the rnd with 1 sl st in the first ch of the rnd.

Rnd 34: 1 ch= the first dc of the rnd. *`3 ch, in the joining st of the flower, work 1 leaf/3 dtr + 7 ch + 1 leaf/3 dtr, 3 ch, 1 dc in the dc from the previous rnd. Rep from * the rest of the rnd, finish after the last leaf of the rnd by working 1 tr in the first ch of the rnd.

Rnd 35: 4 ch, work 1 leaf/2 dtr in the top of the tr from the previous rnd without finishing = 3 loops + *1 leaf/3 dtr in the top of the next leaf from the previous rnd, yo and pull through all 6 loops on the hook, 3 ch, 1 dc in the 4th of the 7 ch, 3 ch, work 1 leaf/3 dtr in the top of the next leaf without finishing = 3 loops on the hook*. Rep from *-* the rest of the rnd, finish off with 1 sl st in the 4th ch of the rnd.

Rnd 36: Work 3 ch = 1 tr, *2 tr around the ch loop, 1 tr in the 2 leaves. Rep from *, finish the rnd with 1 sl st in the 3rd ch from the beg of the rnd = 324 tr.

Rnd 37 – 57: 3 ch = 1 tr, *2 ch, miss 2 st, 1 tr in the next st, rep from * the rest of the rnd = 108 meshes, finish the rnd with 1 sl st in the 3rd ch of the rnd.

Rnd 58: 3 ch, continue with 1 tr over all st, finish off with 1 sl st in the 3rd ch from the beg of the rnd. Break the thread and fasten off.

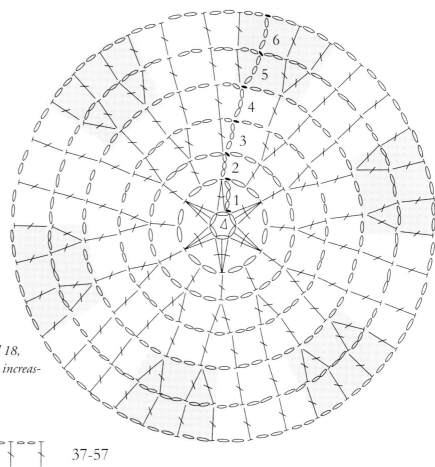

Diagram 1.
The diagram shows the increases for the
bottom of the backpack. The grey areas
indicate the places where the increases are
made, repeated in the same place until rnd 18,
meaning that there is a total of 7 rnds with increas-
ing = 108 meshes in rnd 18.

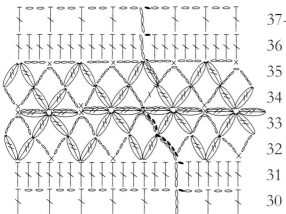

37-57
36
35
34
33
32
31
30

Diagram 2. Work straight up from rnd 18 – 30 without
increasing. The insertion is worked after rnd 30. Work straight
up from rnd 37 –57.

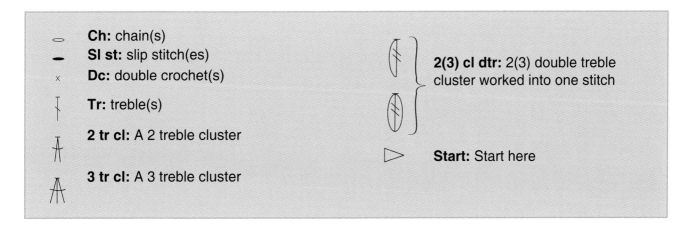

  ⊖   **Ch:** chain(s)
  ▬   **Sl st:** slip stitch(es)
  ×   **Dc:** double crochet(s)

     Tr: treble(s)

     2 tr cl: A 2 treble cluster

     3 tr cl: A 3 treble cluster

2(3) cl dtr: 2(3) double treble
cluster worked into one stitch

▷   **Start:** Start here

31

Passementerie string

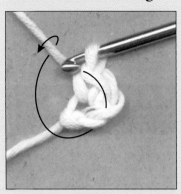

Work 2 ch, then 1 dc in the 2nd ch from the hook, stitch down around 2 loops.

*Thus turning the string a ½ round (away from yourself).

The thread must remain at the back of the work all the time…

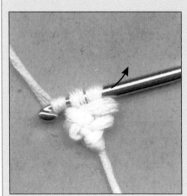

… yo the hook pull through 2 loops = 2 remaining loops on the hook. Yo and pull through the 2 remaining loops on the hook…

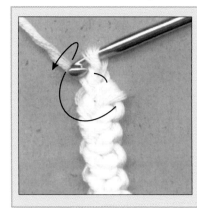

… stitch down around 2 loops. Rep from * until the string has reached the required length.

Work 2 strings measuring approx 80 cm.

Crocheted straps

Work 1 strap in the 1st inc in rnds 18 and 19.
Row 1: Fasten the thread with 1 sl st in the tr, 3 ch = 1 tr, work 6 tr over 2 meshes.
Row 2 – 6: 3 ch = 1 tr, 6 tr. Break the thread and sew the edge of the strap onto the 1st row of tr.
Work a strap similar to the first one on the opposite side in the 4th inc in rnd 18 and 19.

Place the strings: Pull 1 string through rnd 5 and 1 string the opposite way through rnd 7 from above, alternating over and under 9 meshes. Put one string through one strap and the other string down through the other strap. Sew the ends together with invisible stitches.

Summery bag made of Granny squares

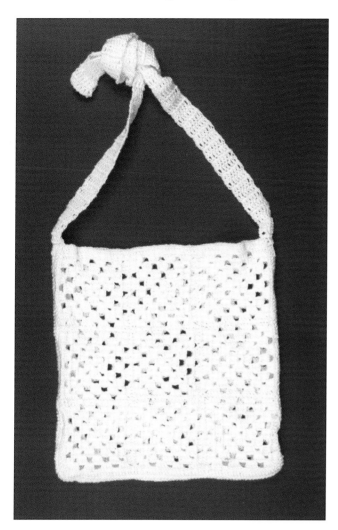

Mounting

Make sure that all of the squares are the same side up. Sew the squares together from the front (see detail photo). Place 2 squares with front against front. Start at the corner, stab the needle down in the middle of the crossing loop of the stitches on both squares and sew tog with whip stitches. Sew the next 2 squares tog without breaking the thread in the same way. First sew all the vertical hems tog and then all the horizontal ones until 9 squares are sewn tog. Sew the other 9 squares tog the same way.

This pretty little bag might quickly turn into your favourite. It is made of 18 pieces of Granny squares, worked in the same colour. The strap of the bag is worked in trebles. The bag is lined and thus the pattern is enhanced.

Dimensions: Approx 19 x 20 cm
Materials: Approx 100 white Petra no. 5 from DMC. Running length approx 420 m/100 g. Crochet hook no. 2.

Tension: 1 square is 6 x 6 cm.

Square

Make 6 ch and form a ring with 1 sl st worked into the first ch. Follow the diagram. Make a total of 18 squares.

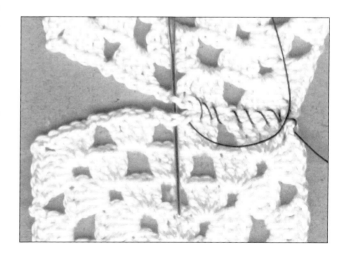

Here you can see the joining with whip stitches.

Working over edges

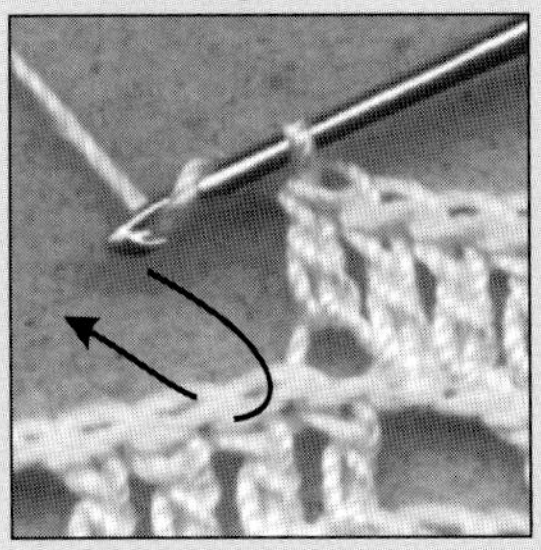

Work an edge with tr over the 3 sides on each part. Fasten the thread with 1 sl st in one of the corners, 3 ch and work 1 tr in back loop of each st, on all 3 sides. Make edges on the other part of the bag the same way.

Joining

Place the 2 parts for the bag front against front and work the parts tog with dc by putting the hook the tr of both layers and working 1 dc, cont until you have finished all 3 edges.

Upper edge of the bag

Then work the upper edge of the bag. Work tr in the back loops the rest of the round, 1 tr in each st.

Strap for bag

Work 9 ch.

Rnd 1: beg in the 3rd ch from the hook, work tr the rest of the row.

Rnd 2: Turn with 3 ch = 1 tr in the row, work 6 tr over 6 tr. Rep rnd 2 until the strap is 90 cm or the length you want it to be.
Sew the strap onto the sides of the bag with invisible stitches.

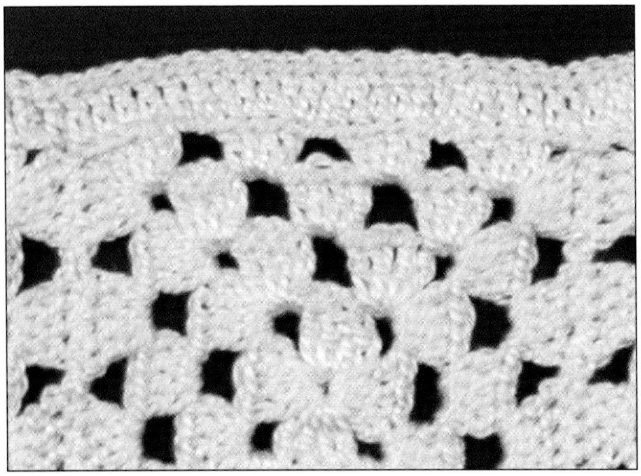

Linen for bag

Cut a piece of fabric 22 x 42 cm, fold it on the long side and sew the sides tog. Place the linen in the bag. Fold the upper edge of the linen down until it fits at the beg of the tr rows on the bag, sew the linen on the bag with invisible stitches.

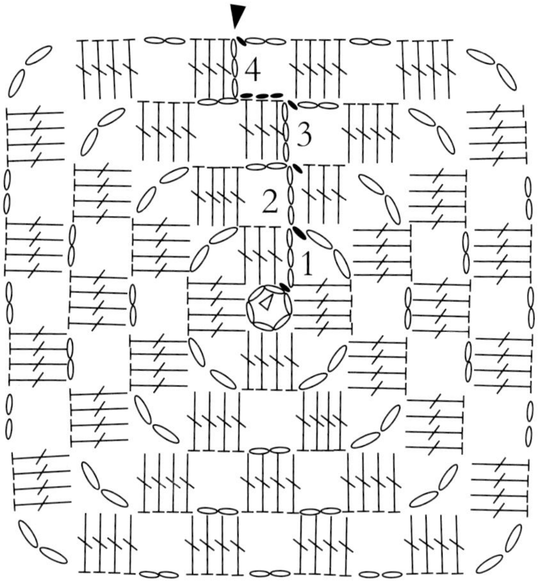

Diagram for Granny squares. Work 4 rnds. You need 18 squares for the bag.

Tips about Granny squares
This is a classic motif. It is known as pattern where you may use your leftover yarn. Meaning a new colour for each row. But Granny squares also look good in one colour. Once you have learned the technique, it is easy to make a pram cover or even a larger blanket. You can make approx 50 squares from 100 g Petra no. 5 from DMC.

- ⬭ **Ch:** chain(s)
- ▬ **Sl st:** slip stitch(es)
- ⫲ **Tr:** treble(s)
- ▷ **Start:** Start here
- ▶ **End:** End here

Small round purse

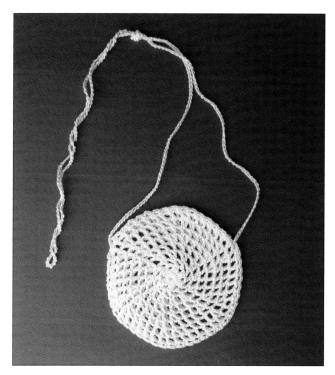

A small but very useful purse to hang around your neck – then you can always find your small change.

Dimension: diameter 7 cm.

Materials: Approx 50 g white Cebelia no. 20 from DMC. Running length approx 380 m/50 g. Crochet hook no. 1.25.

Tension: 8 rnds = 7 cm.

2(3) treble cluster: (yo, insert hook in st, yo and pull through st, yo and pull through 2 loops) 2(3) times, yo and pull through the last 3(4) loops = 2(3) treble cluster.

Round purse
Work 6 ch and close the ring with 1 sl st in the 1 st ch of the rnd.

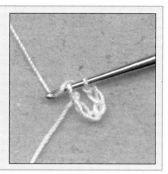

Rnd 1: Work 3 ch = 1 tr , work 2 tr cl in the ring…

… 2 ch, (3 tr cl, 2 ch) 5 times…

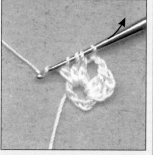

Finish the round by working 1 sl st in the 3rd ch from the beg of the rnd.

Follow the diagram. Work 8 rnds. Break the thread. Make another similar part.

Mounting
Place the two parts with the wrong sides together and crochet them together. Insert the hook through both layers at once and work *1 dc in tr, 2 ch, miss 2 ch. Rep from *, leave 15 meshes for opening, rep

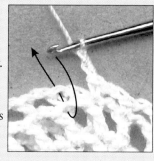

from * but only through a single layer, finish the rnd with 1 sl st in the first ch. Continue working a string of ch without breaking the thread, make the string 70 cm or the length you prefer. Fasten the string with a sl st on the opposite side of the opening of the purse. Break the thread and fasten off.

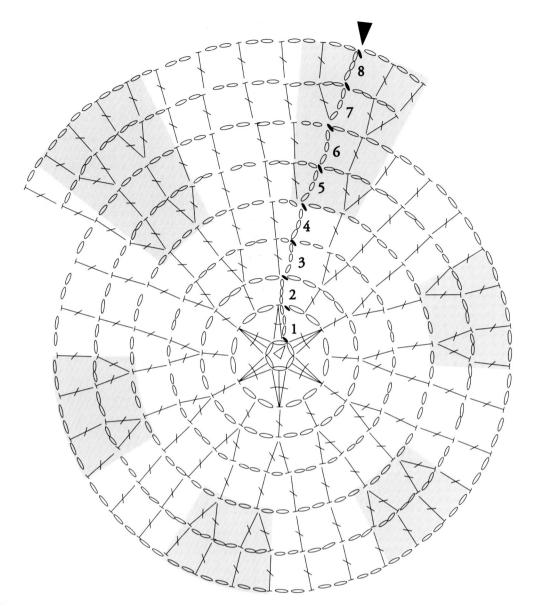

Diagram for round purse. The grey areas indicate, where to make the increases. These are repeated in the same place through the work. Work a total of 8 rnds. The first 6 rnds are shown completely. Rnd 7 and 8 are only partially shown.

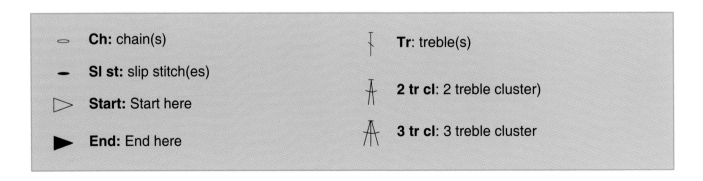

Ch: chain(s)

Sl st: slip stitch(es)

▷ **Start:** Start here

▶ **End:** End here

Tr: treble(s)

2 tr cl: 2 treble cluster)

3 tr cl: 3 treble cluster

Airy summer tank top

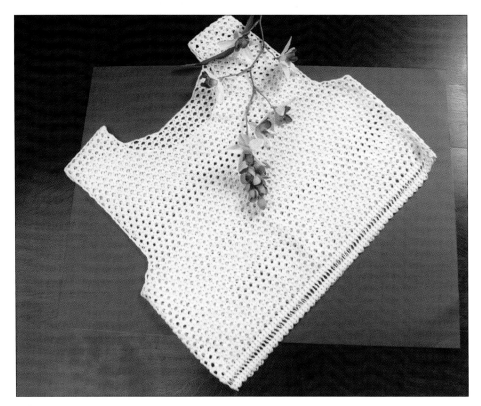

This pretty, airy summer tank top may attract some attention. The lower lace border is worked across. The pattern is worked on top of the lace.

Size: S(M)L.

Dimensions: see chart.

Materials: Approx 200(250)300 g white Babylo no. 20/12 from DMC. Running length approx 400 m/50 g. Crochet hook no. 1.25.

Tension: (4 tr + 2 ch = 1 tr gr). 8 tr grs and 20 rnds = 10 x 10 cm. To obtain the best possible quality for your top it is important to maintain the tension. If it does not fit, please try with a finer or thicker hook.

Lace border
See diagram 1
Row 1: Work 11 ch. Work 3 tr + 2 ch + 4 tr in the 4th ch from the hook, 4 ch, miss 6 ch, work 4 tr + 2 ch + 4 tr in the last st.

Row 2: Turn the work with 3 ch, in the 2 ch arc work 4 tr + 2 ch + 4 tr.
Rep row 2 until the lace reaches the required length.

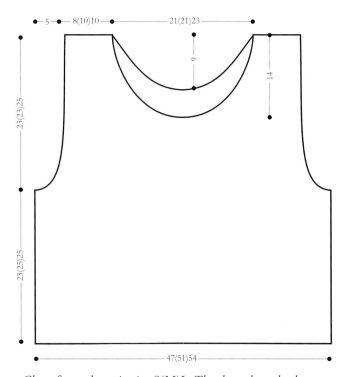

Chart for tank top in size S(M)L. The chart shows back + front. All measurements are made in cm.

38

Tank top pattern

See diagram 1. Fasten the thread with 1 sl st at the arrow.

Row 1: 3 ch, 3 tr in ch arch, *2 ch, 4 tr in the next ch arch, rep from * the rest of the row.

Row 2: 1 ch *4 tr in the ch arch with 2 ch, rep from * the rest of the row, finish off with 1 sl st in the 3rd ch from the previous row.

Row 3: 8 ch *4 tr in the 2 ch arch, 2 ch, rep from * the rest of the row, finish the row with a triple tr in the 1st ch from the previous row.

Row 4: 5 ch, 4 tr in the 2 first ch, * work 4 tr + 2 ch + 4 tr in the next ch arch, rep from * the rest of the row.

The rows 2 – 4 constitutes the pattern and is rep throughout the work.

Back

Work the lace a total of 78(84)90 rows. Then fasten on the thread at the edge as shown in diagram 1 with a sl st, work 3 tr in the 1st ch arch, 2 ch, work 2 ch + 4 tr in the next ch arch, continue until the amount of tr grs reach 39(42)45. Continue straight up according to the diagram until row 37(41)41, where the armhole is made, see diagram 2. Then work straight up until row 67(71)75. Form the neck in the left side, see diagram 3 regarding dec for neck, work ½ + 11(12)13 scallops (scallop = 4 tr + 2 ch + 4 tr) + 1 tr in the next ch arch, finish the neck according to the diagram. Miss 6(6)7 tr grs at the neckline , fasten the thread with 1 sl st, work the other part of the neckline according to the diagram.

Front

Worked the same way as the back until row 59(63)69, where the neckband is made, work the left part after diagram 3. Miss 6(6)7 tr grs, fasten the thread at the edge with 1 sl st and work the right side of the neckline according to diagram 3.

Mounting

Crochet the shoulder seam tog over 6(7)7 + ½ scallops. Replace the 2 ch with 2 sl st in the last row of the front piece. See diagram 4 regarding joining the shoulder seams. Sew the side of the tank top tog with whip stitches.

Borders

Work 1 rnd of dc over every st along the neckline and shoulder hole. Take care the edges do not philander.

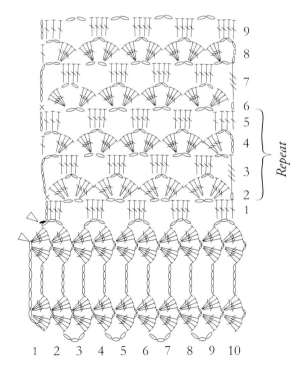

Diagram 1. The pattern for the tank top consists of a crossing lace whereto a pattern of chain archs are worked. The parenthesis forms the pattern and is repeated throughout the work.

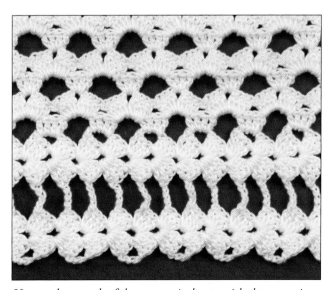

Here a photograph of the pattern is shown with the traversing lace. It forms a beautiful unity with the rest of the pattern on the tank top.

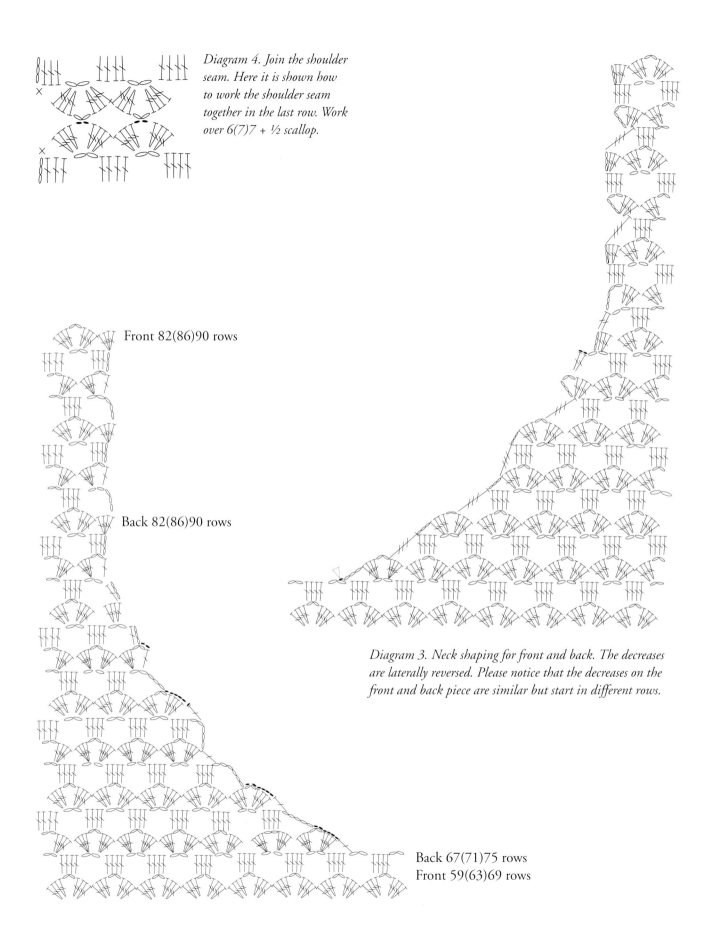

Diagram 4. Join the shoulder seam. Here it is shown how to work the shoulder seam together in the last row. Work over 6(7)7 + ½ scallop.

Front 82(86)90 rows

Back 82(86)90 rows

Diagram 3. Neck shaping for front and back. The decreases are laterally reversed. Please notice that the decreases on the front and back piece are similar but start in different rows.

Back 67(71)75 rows
Front 59(63)69 rows

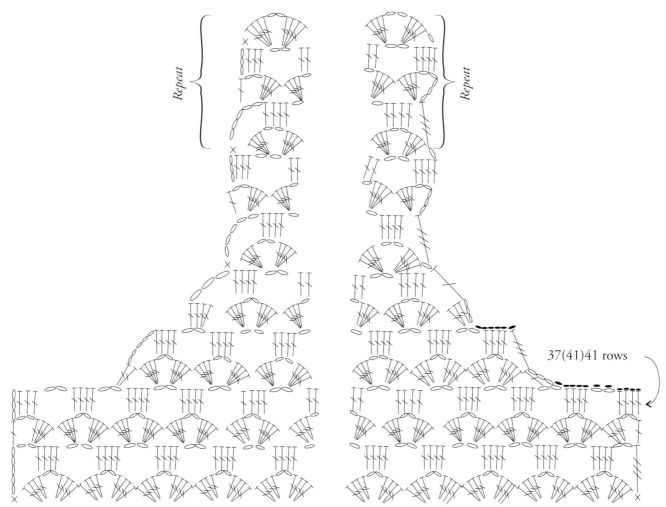

Diagram 2. Armopening. Here the decreases for the armopening are shown – it is formed over 4 rows.

37(41)41 rows

Tips – change of thread.

It looks best if the thread is replaced at the beginning of a row. But if this is not possible you will have to make it as invisible as possible. The best result is obtained when there are 2 loops left on the hook, the new yarn over the hook that is pulled through the 2 loops on the hook, continue working as usual. The loose ends of thread are fastened at the back of the work as invisible as possible when the work is finished.

⬭ **Ch:** chain(s)

▬ **Sl st:** slip stitch(es)

× **Dc:** double crochet(s)

† **Tr:** treble(s)

‡ **Ttr:** triple treble

▷ **Start:** Start here

Cap with lace

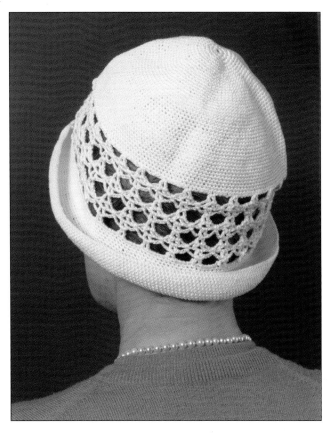

This is a cute and summery cap with a lace insertion. The cap is worked with double crochet, only the part with lace is worked in a treble pattern combination.

Dimensions: Approx 23 cm high, approx 54 cm round.

Materials: Approx 10 g white Petra no. 5 from DMC. Running length approx 420 m/100 g. Crochet hook no. 2.

Tension: 17 dc x 20 rnds = 5 cm.

Decreasing 1 stitch

Decrease 1 dc by working 2 dc in the same st from the previous rnd.

Cap

Work 6 ch and form them to a ring with 1 sl st in the 1st ch.

Rnd 1: Work 12 dc in the ring, continue working around. Place a contrasting thread so you can see where a new rnd starts.

Rnd 2: Work 2 dc in each st = 24 dc.

Rnd 3: Dec in every 2nd st where you work 2 dc = 36 dc.

Rnds 4 – 5: No inc.

Rnd 6: Work 2 dc in every 3rd dc = 48 dc.

Rnds 7 – 8: No inc.

Rnd 9: Work 2 dc in every 4th st

Rnd 10: Work 2 dc in every 5th st = 60 dc.

Rnds 11 – 12: No inc.

Rnd 13: Work 2 dc in every 6th st = 84 dc.

Rnd 14: Work 2 dc in every 7th st = 96 dc.

Rnds 15 – 16: No inc.

Rnd 17: Work 2 dc in every 7th st = 128 dc.

Rnd 18: Work 2 dc in every 7th st = 144 dc.

Rnds 19 – 25: No inc.

Rnd 26: Work 2 dc in every 8th st = 158 dc.

Rnd 27: No inc.

Rnd 28: Work dc in every 10th st = 158 dc.

Rnds 29 –30: No inc.

Rnd 31: Work 2 dc in every 9th st = 175 dc.

Rnds 32 – 42: No inc.

Rnd 43: Continue working the lace pattern according to the diagram.

Rnds 43 – 45 forms the pattern and is repeated 3 times totally.

Rnd 52: Work 1 sl st over the 1st ch, 5 ch, *1 dc in the ch between the tr from the previous rnd, 4 ch. Rep from * the rest of the rnd, finish with 1 sl st in the 1st ch of the rnd.

Rnd 53: Work 1 dc in every st = 175 dc.

Rnds 54 – 57: No inc.

Rnd 58: Work 2 dc in every 9th st = 192 dc.

Rnds 59 – 61: No inc.

Rnd 62: Work 2 dc in every 10th st = 211 dc.

Rnd 63: No inc.

Rnd 64: Work 2 dc in every 10th st = 232 dc.

Rnds 65 – 74: No inc.

Rnd 75: Work sl st in the back loop in this rnd.

Break the thread and fasten off.

Here you see the pretty lace pattern in the cap.

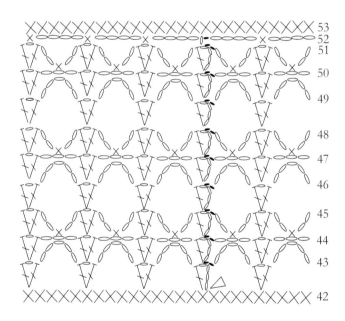

Diagram for the pattern insertion of the cap. The pattern consists of 3 rounds that are repeated 3 times totally. The arrow indicates the beginning of the round and indicates as well how each round is finished with slip stitches.

⌒	**Ch:** chain(s)		⌡	**Tr:** treble(s)
▬	**Sl st:** slip stitch(es)			
×	**Dc:** double crochet(s)		▷	**Start:** Start here

Baby jacket

This fine and airy baby jacket is easy to put on as it only has one button. There are almost no seams in the jacket because the front and back are made in one piece. The shoulders are joined.

Size: 60(70)90 cm.

Dimensions: see chart.

Materials: Approx 100 g Petra no. 8 from DMC. Crochet hook no. 1.25. Sewing needle without a tip.

Tension: 6 pattern grs and 21 rows = 10 x 10 cm. It is very important to maintain the correct tension throughout the work in order for the finished work to look good.

If the tension does not match, you have to try a finer or thicker hook.

Pattern: See diagram 1. For example work 40 ch for a test.

Row 1: Work 1 tr + 2 ch + 2 tr in the 4th ch from the hook, *5 ch, miss 5 ch, work 2 tr + 2 ch + 2 tr in the next st, rep from *.

Row 2: Work 2 sl st in 2 tr, 3 ch, work 1 tr + 2 ch + 2 tr in the 2 ch from the previous rnd, * 2 ch, 1 dc around the 5 ch from previous rnd, 2 ch, work 2 tr + 2 ch + 2 tr in the next 2 ch, rep from *.

Row 3: work 2 sl st over 2 tr, 3 ch, work 1 tr + 2 ch + 2 tr

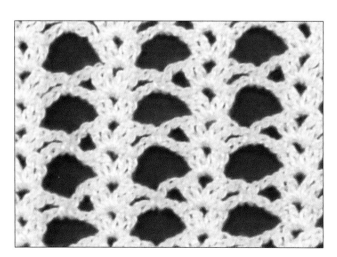

Detail photo for lace pattern on baby jacket.

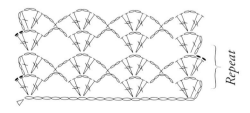

Diagram 1. Pattern for baby jacket. Rows 2 and 3 forms the pattern and is repeated.

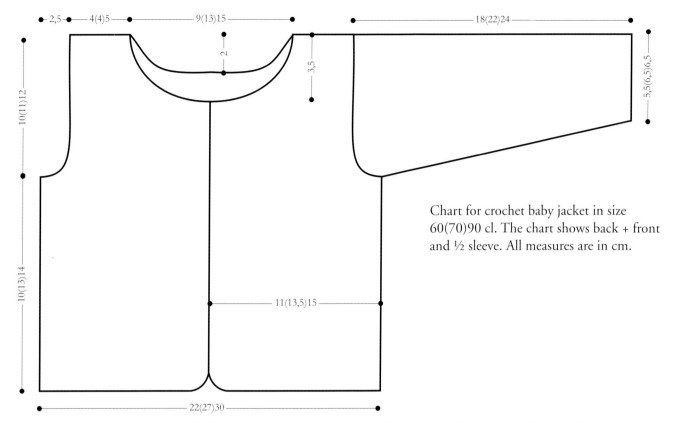

Chart for crochet baby jacket in size 60(70)90 cl. The chart shows back + front and ½ sleeve. All measures are in cm.

in the 2 ch from the previous rnd, *5 ch, miss 9 ch, work 2 tr + 2 ch + 2 tr in the next 2 ch, rep from*.

Rows 2 – 3 forms the pattern and is repeated throughout the work.

Front and back piece

Work 184(208)232 ch and make the pattern according to diagram 1 = 30(34)38 pattern grs. Work straight up until the work is 10(13)14 cm = 19(25)27 rows.

Split the work in 3 parts, first work the left front, then the right and at last the back where the work is divided one more time – work the left part of the neckband first and then the right part.

Make the arm shaping of the left front: Work 7(8)9 pattern grs + 1 tr in the 5 ch arch. Work the rest of the arm shaping according to diagram 2.

Continue straight up until the work is 18(22)24 cm = 31(25)43 rows and the start the dec for the neck shaping. Work the pattern over 5(5)6 pattern grs, form the neck over 9 rows according to diagram 3, Break the thread in row 38(44)52.

The armopening on the right front is worked in the same way just laterally reversed, see diagram 2, miss 16(18)20 pattern grs and fasten the thread with 1 sl st in the next ch arch, as shown in diagram 2. Work 18(19)19 sl st in row 33(36)44 until reaching the arrow at the right front in diagram 3, continue according to the diagram.

Diagram 2. Arm shaping for front pieces and back.

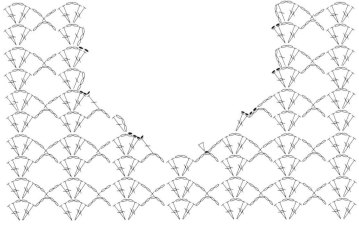

19(25)27 rows

Back

Miss 1 pattern gr, fasten the thread at the edge with 1 sl st and work the dec for the arm shaping after the diagram, work straight up until the work is 18(22)24 cm = 33(39)47 rows. First make the left side of the neck shaping, work after the diagram. Then miss 2(4)4 pattern grs and fasten the thread in the right side of the neck, which now must be finished.

Please notice that in the last row on the back the 2 ch are replaced with 2 sl st for joining the shoulder seam. See diagram 4. Join them from the front.

Sleeve

Make 58(64)64 ch, work inc in both sides of the sleeve. See diagram 5 regarding inc for sleeve edges, rep the parenthesis twice – 4 rows(+ 4 rows)+ 10 rows, work straight up = 29(37)47 rows = 13(14)14 pattern grs.

Then work dec over the following 6 rows for sleeve cap, see diagram 6 for sleeve rounding = 5(6)6 pattern grs. Break the thread and work another sleeve the same way.

Button

6 ch, work 16 dc in the ring, continue working in rounds. Work 1 rnd with 1 dc in each st, work dc tog in pairs = 8 dc, pull the thread through the rest of the st = 1 button.

Mounting

Join the shoulder seam. Sew the edges of the sleeve tog and sew the sleeves on front and back with whip stitches. Sew a button just opposite of the bar.

Borders

Work a border on the edges of the sleeves and the below edge in 1 rnd like this: Fasten the thread at the edge with 1 sl st, * 7 dc in the ch arch and 1 dc in the tr gr, rep from *.

Neckline

Rnd 1: Fasten the thread at the right side of the edge with 1 sl st, * 7 dc in the ch arch, 1 dc in the tr gr, rep from *.

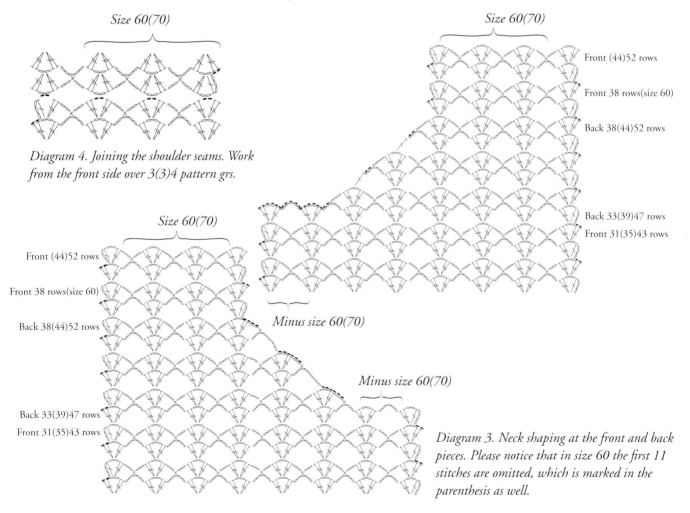

Diagram 4. Joining the shoulder seams. Work from the front side over 3(3)4 pattern grs.

Diagram 3. Neck shaping at the front and back pieces. Please notice that in size 60 the first 11 stitches are omitted, which is marked in the parenthesis as well.

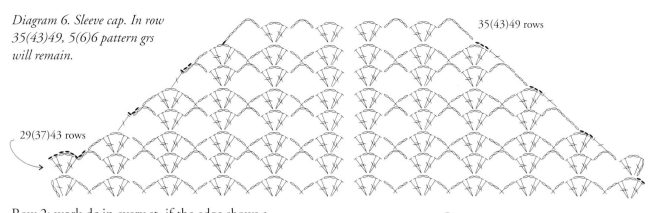

Diagram 6. Sleeve cap. In row 35(43)49, 5(6)6 pattern grs will remain.

35(43)49 rows

29(37)43 rows

Row 2: work dc in every st, if the edge shows a tendency to philander, then work dec (2 dc tog) distributed around the neck shaping.

Work 15 ch at the end of row 2, fasten with 1 sl st in the 1st rnd of the 1st sl st of the neck shaping, turn the work and work 20 dc back over the ch arch.

Row 3: work dc in each st. Break the thread, fasten the ends.

Minus size 60

Repeated twice.

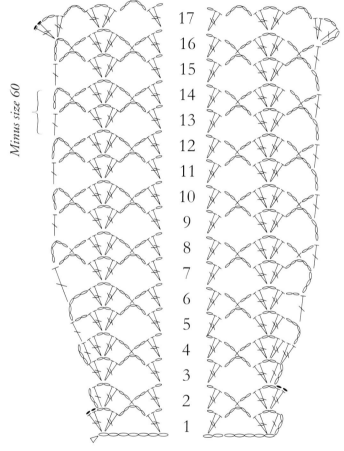

17
16
15
14
13
12
11
10
9
8
7
6
5
4
3
2
1

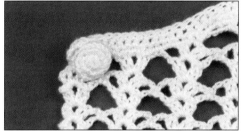

Detail photo of button worked in double crochet.

Detail photo of crochet bar at the neck shaping.

Tips. Which side is right and which side is left?
It may sometimes seem a bit confusing when a chart, for a jacket for example, shows the right front piece (even though the drawing shows the left side).

But then you just have to think about when the clothing is worn, then the left front piece turns out to be the correct side after all. Remember that drawings as well as recipes always refer to the finished work.

⌒	**Ch:** chain(s)
▬	**Sl st:** slip stitch(es)
×	**Dc:** double crochet(s)
⊤	**Tr:** treble(s)
▷	**Start:** Start here

Flower doily

Despite its size, this lovely six-sided flower doily is fairly difficult to make.

Dimensions: Widest place 14 x 14 cm.

Materials: Approx 50 g white Babylo no. 20/12 from DMC. Running length approx 400 m/50 g. Crochet hook no. 1.25.

Tension: 1 flower = 2.5 cm x 2.5 cm.
It is very important to maintain the tension throughout the work in order to obtain a satisfying end result. If the tension does not fit, you will have to use a finer or thicker hook.

1 leaf
Work 2(3)4 ttr in the same st like this: yo 3 times, insert the hook in the st, yo and pull through 1 loop, (yo, pull through 2 loops) 3 times, yo and pull the thread through all 3(4)5 loops on the hook = 1 leaf.
The leaves in rnds 1, 3, 4, 5 and 6 are worked like this.

Flower doily
Work 6 ch and form a ring with 1 sl st in the 1st ch. Follow the diagram and the photo for that particular rnd.

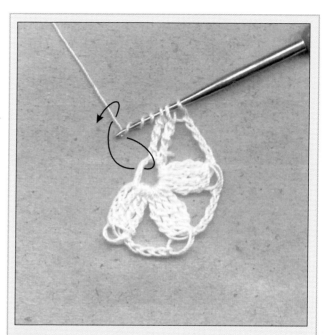

Rnd 1: Work 5 ch, 1 leaf = 3 ttr in the ring, (5 ch, 4 ttr in the ring) 5 times, 5 ch, finish the rnd with 1 sl st in the 5th ch from the beg of the rnd.

Rnd 2: Work 5 ch, ttr at the top of the next leaf...

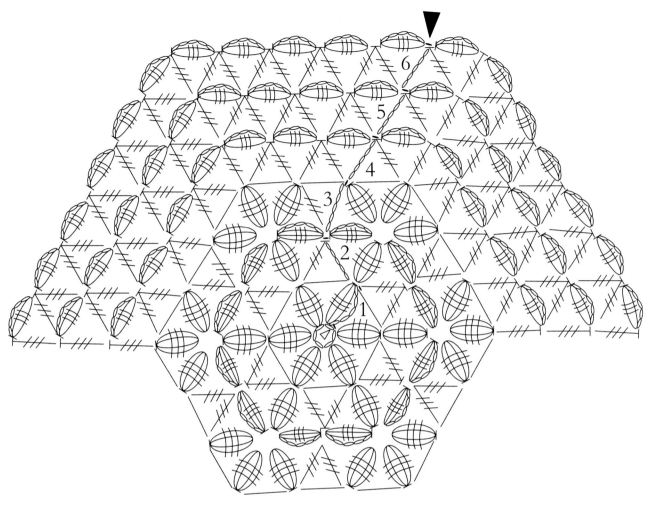

Diagram for the six-sided flower doily.
The first 3 rounds of the diagram are completely shown. Rounds 4 – 6 are only partially shown.

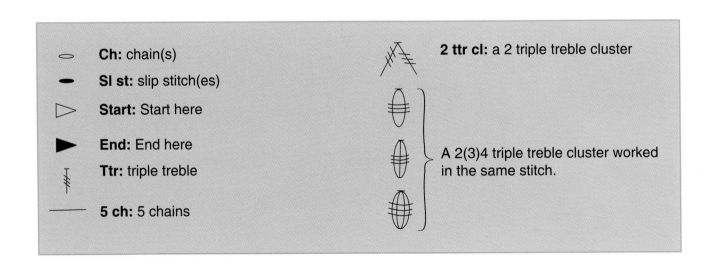

Ch: chain(s)

Sl st: slip stitch(es)

Start: Start here

End: End here

Ttr: triple treble

5 ch: 5 chains

2 ttr cl: a 2 triple treble cluster

A 2(3)4 triple treble cluster worked in the same stitch.

… * 5 ch, 1 leaf = 3 ttr in the ttr, but without finishing the leaf (step 1) = 4 loops on the hook.

… yo and pull the thread through all of the 8 loops at the same time…

Work a new leaf = 4 ttr worked in the same st as the ttr worked in = 8 loops on the hook.

… work 5 ch, then 1 leaf = 3 ttr in the same stitch the 7 ttr was worked in, yo and pull through all of the 4 loops.

Work ttr in the 1st leaf + ttr in the next leaf, yo and pull through all of the 3 loops on the hook at the same time. Rep from * the rest of the rnd, finish the rnd after the last 3 worked leaves with 1 sl st worked in the 5th ch from the beg of the rnd.

Rnd 3: Work 10 ch, * ttr in the sl st from the previous rnd, 1 leaf = 4 ttr worked in the cl st of the 2 leaves from the previous rnd + 5 ch + 1 leaf + 5 ch + 1 leaf ...

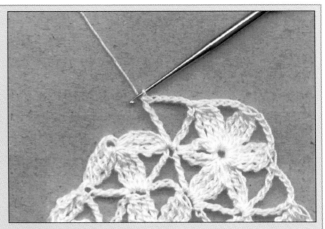

... work ttr + 5 ch + 3 dtr in the 2 ttr cl from the previous rnd, rep from * - *, finish with 1 sl st in the 5th ch from the beg of the rnd after the 3rd leaf.

Rnd 4 – 6: Work 10 ch, 1 leaf = 2 ttr in the 5th ch...

...work 2 ttr cl at the top of the next 2 leaves.

52

Please notice about the stitches in the corner - the 2nd leaf in the flower from the previous rnd – work an extra leaf + 3 ttr as shown in this photo.

Repeat from *, finish the rnd with 1 sl st worked in the 5th ch from the beg of the rnd after the ttr.

Break the thread and fasten off.

Round doily

This almost spidery doily consists of chains only. It looks very beautiful on a dark wooden tabletop.

Dimensions: Diameter 20 cm.

Materials: Approx 20 g white Cordonnet Special no. 20 from DMC. Running length approx 160 m/20 g. Crochet hook no. 1.25.

Round doily

Follow the diagram. Work 10 ch, form a ring with 1 sl st in the 1st ch of the rnd.

> **Tips.** It is easy to make the doily larger by repeating rounds 6 – 9 until the doily obtains the required size, then make the finishing edge.

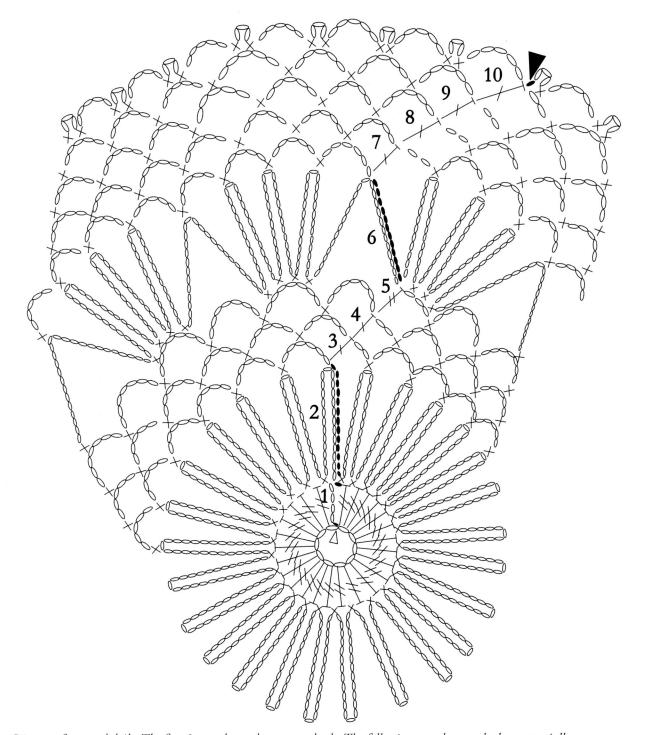

Diagram for round doily. The first 2 rounds are shown completely. The following rounds are only shown partially.

�⌐ **Ch:** chain(s)		**Dtr:** double treble
Sl st: slip stitch(es)		
× **Dc:** double crochet(s)	▷	**Start:** Start here
Tr: treble(s)	►	**End:** End here

Classic doily

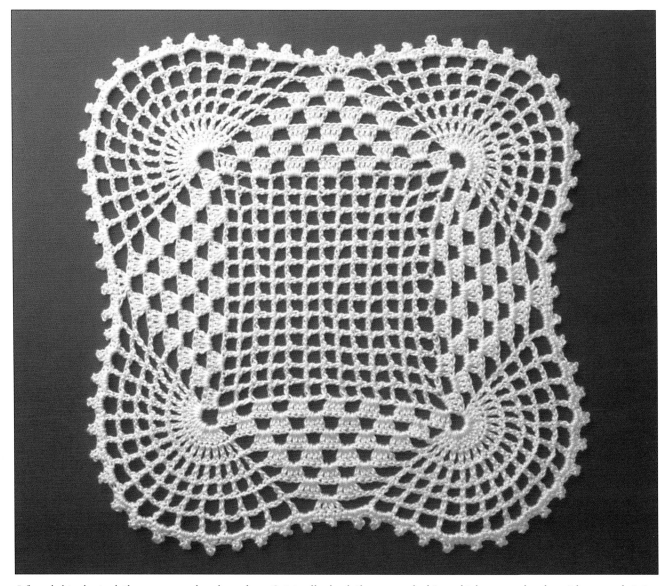

I found this classic doily at my grandmothers place. Originally the doily was worked in a thicker yarn, but here I have made it in a much more elegant version.

Dimensions: Approx 15 x 15 cm.

Materials: Approx 20 g white Cordonnet Special no. 20 from DMC. Running length approx 160 m/20 g. Crochet hook 1.25.

Tension: 30 st x 10 rows = 5 x 5 cm.

Doily: Make 42 ch. Start in the 8th from the hook with 1 tr. Follow the diagram.

Continue working the edge without breaking the thread. See how rnd 1 is worked at page 58. Continue working from the diagram.

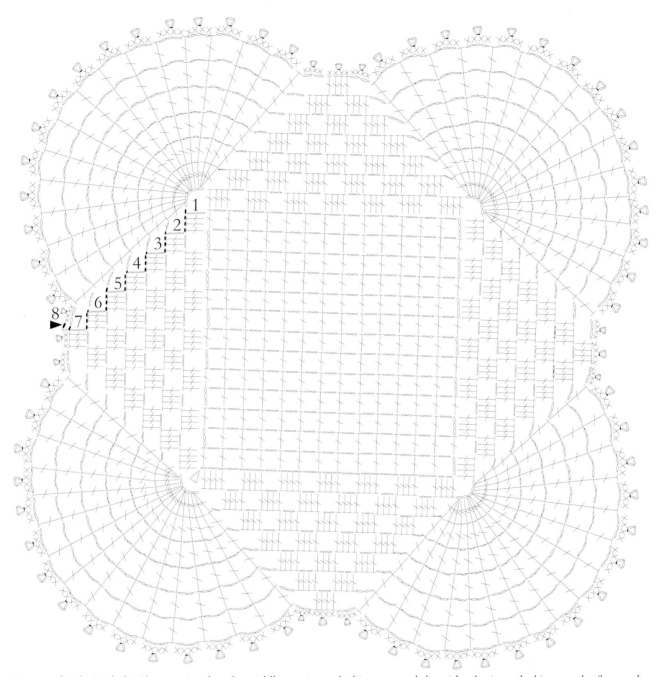

Diagram for classic doily. Please notice that the middle part is worked in rows and the wide edge is worked in rounds afterwards. The picots are worked on the last round. Start at the arrow.

⌒	**Ch:** chain(s)	▷	**Start:** Start here
▬	**Sl st:** slip stitch(es)	▶	**End:** End here
×	**Dc:** double crochet(s)		
⟊	**Tr:** treble(s)		

How to make round 1

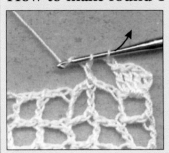

Continue working around the edge of the work without breaking the thread, work 3 st and 3 tr over the tr, *(2 tr, miss 3 ch at the edge

..and work 4 tr over the next tr) 6 times, 5 ch + 4 tr in the edge arch. Rep from *.

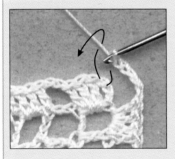

Finish with 1 sl st worked the 3rd ch from the beg of the rnd. Continue working according to the diagram.

How to make the picot edge

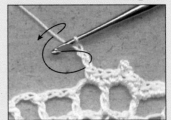

Start the round with 1 chain replacing the slip stitch, 1 double crochet, * 3 chains, 1 slip stitch in the 3rd ch from the hook = 1 picot...

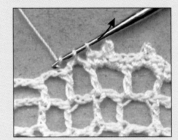

... 4 double crochet over 4 stitches. Repeat from *, finish with 1 slip stitch in the 1st chain from the beginning of the round. Break the thread and fasten off.

Tips about stretching the work.

When you have finished the work, it may turn out to be an advantage to wet the work and while it is still wet, stretch the work out in shape to make it smooth and even. Stretch the work according to the measures stated in the recipe. Place rustless pins in every round or arch, the more pins the better. Make sure that all details are straightened out, this means that picots and edges are straightened out with pins remaining in the work until it is completely dry.

Doily with star-shaped motif

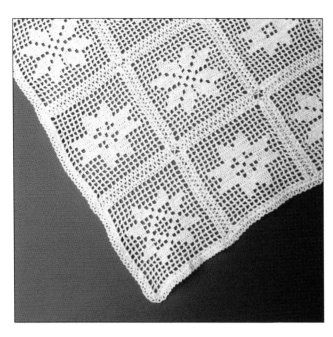

The beautiful doily with star motif will look good on every table. The pattern is made from 4 different stars worked in filet crochet. All of the squares are combined to an entity and with a fine thin edge. A lovely needle work.

Dimensions: Approx 170 x 170 cm.

Materials: Approx 650 g white Babylo no. 20/12 from DMC. Running length approx 400 m/50 g. Crochet hook no. 1.25.

Tension: 1 square without the treble edging is 10 x 10 cm. It is very important to maintain the tension throughout the work in order to obtain a satisfying end result. If the tension does not fit, you will have to use a finer or thicker hook.

Motif 1: Make 56 ch.
Follow the diagram.

Make the treble edging around each square like this: fasten the thread in the corner with 1 sl st, work 3 ch, * 2 tr around each ch arch, rep from *, work 7 tr in the corner arch, continue working the rest of the rnd, finish the rnd with 1 sl st in the 3rd ch from the beg of the rnd.

Please notice that there is no treble edge on the square edges on the outer side of the doily. This goes for 4 x 12 motives. See the chart,

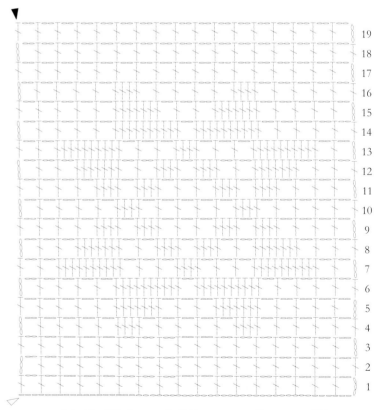

Motif 1. Work a total of 43 stars according to motif 1.

Regarding which side of the square not to make the treble edge on.

When all of the motives are joined then work a finishing treble edge around the complete doily.

Motif 2, 3 and 4: Work 56 ch, start in the 8th ch from the hook. Follow the diagrams.

Amount of squares: 42 squares with motif 2. 42 squares with motif 3. 42 squares with motif 4.

Joining the doily: place the squares as shown on the chart. First join all horizontal seams so all the squares are connected. Then join all the vertical hems.

Make sure that all of the squares are facing the front side upwards.

The squares are joined from the front side with a slightly elastic zigzag seam. Place 2 squares opposite each other and start joining at the corner. Work in the space (see diagram on page 62) between the trs.

Horizontal seams: Follow the diagram. Fasten the thread with 1 sl st in the 3rd ch of the 1st square, 1 sl st between 1st and 2nd tr, 3 ch, miss 2 tr on square 1, 1 sl st, 3 ch, miss 2 tr

1	2	3	4	1	2	3	4	1	2	3	4	1
4	1	2	3	4	1	2	3	4	1	2	3	4
3	4	1	2	3	4	1	2	3	4	1	2	3
2	3	4	1	2	3	4	1	2	3	4	1	2
1	2	3	4	1	2	3	4	1	2	3	4	1
4	1	2	3	4	1	2	3	4	1	2	3	4
3	4	1	2	3	4	1	2	3	4	1	2	3
2	3	4	1	2	3	4	1	2	3	4	1	2
1	2	3	4	1	2	3	4	1	2	3	4	1
4	1	2	3	4	1	2	3	4	1	2	3	4
3	4	1	2	3	4	1	2	3	4	1	2	3
2	3	4	1	2	3	4	1	2	3	4	1	2
1	2	3	4	1	2	3	4	1	2	3	4	1

The chart shows how to place the squares. Work a total of 169 squares. 43 with motif, 42 with motif 2, 3 and 4 respectively. The chart also shows which of the squares there is no treble edging on.

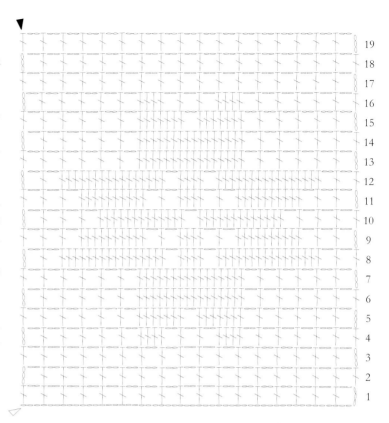

Motif 2. Work a total of 42 squares with motif 2.

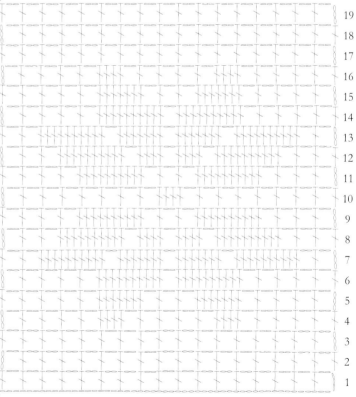

Motif 3. Work a total of 42 squares with motif 3.

On the 2nd square, continue with the zigzag until reaching the 3rd and 4th tr of the opposite corner, 3 ch, 1 dc in the corner of the 3rd square, 3 ch, 1 dc in the 4th square.

Continue with the zigzag over all 13 squares.

All horizontal squares must be worked like this.

Vertical seams are worked like the horizontal seams until the corner, where a small cross is made like this: work 3 ch, 1 dc around the ch arch from the horizontal seam, 3 ch, 1 dc in the st connecting the horizontal seams, * 3 ch, miss 2 st, 1 dc in the next st. Rep from * until the next crossing.

Lace border

Rnd 1: follow the diagram (see diagram on page 63) for the border of the doily.

Break the thread and fasten off.

Stretch the doily with pins according to the stated measures 170 x 170 cm. Iron it under a moist piece of fabric. Leave it until it is completely dry.

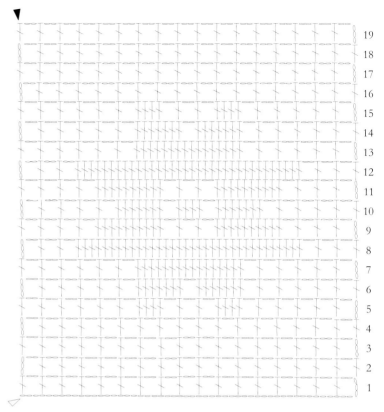

Motif 4. Work a total of 42 squares with motif 4.

Diagram for joining the doily. Start at the arrow. First work the horizontal seams, then work the vertical seams.

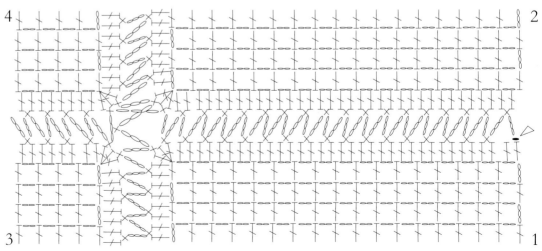

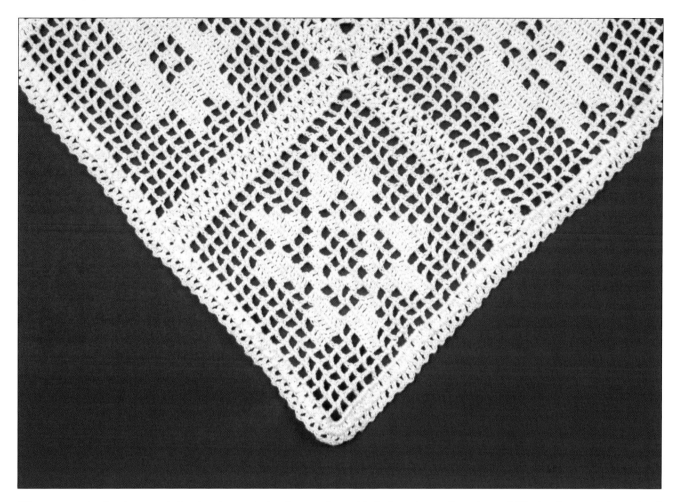

Here you see the fine but simple border that encircles the complete tablecloth with star-shaped motif. The border is simply made of trebles and chains only.

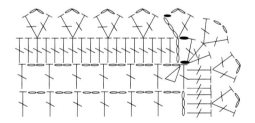

Diagram for the border of the tablecloth. The border is made in 2 rnds.

⌒	**Ch:** chain(s)
▬	**Sl st:** slip stitch(es)
×	**Dc:** double crochet(s)
†	**Tr:** treble(s)
▷	**Start:** Start here
▶	**End:** End here

Patchwork doily

The wide lace border adds lightness to the doily. The rustic linen squares and the fine crochet border creates a beautiful correlation. This is a needlework that you will fall in love with as you watch it growing. You can make the doily whatever size you want to.

Dimensions: 1 square with border is 35 cm.
4 joined squares are approx 70 x 70 cm.
9 joined squares are approx 105 x 105 cm.

Materials: White Babylo no. 20/12 from DMC. The running length is approx 400 m/50 g. Approx 50 g for 4 squares. Approx 100 g for 9 squares. Crochet hook no. 1.25.
Unbleached linen with 12 threads per cm, 1 square is 33 x 33 cm.

Tension: 4 flowers = 5 cm. The edge is approx 3 cm totally.

Preparing the fabric squares: cut out squares measuring 33 x 33 cm. Zigzag the edges to prevent fraying. Fold in the edges reducing the measures to 30 x 30 cm, iron the edges until they are sharp.

The first round, which is worked at the edge of the fabric, is the most difficult to make as it may be a bit difficult to push the hook through the fabric. Insert the crochet hook 3 – 4 threads below the edge.
It may be helpful to mark 3 – 4 support points at the edge, which counts the amount of double stitches you want to make along the fabric edge.

Lace border

Rnd 1: start as shown in the diagram. Work dc over the edges, 180 dc on each edge + 3 dc in each corner.

Continue according to the diagram.

Rnd 2: 6 ch, work 1 tr in the 1st ch from the previous rnd, (3 ch, miss 5 dc, work 1 tr + 3 ch + 1 tr) in the next st 24 times = 25 pattern grs + corner with gr. Continue in the same way the rest of the rnd, finish the rnd after the corner with 3 ch, 1 sl st in the 3rd ch from the beg of the rnd.

▷ **Start:** Start here	× **Dc:** double crochet(s)
▶ **End:** End here	**3 dc:** 3 double crochet in the same stitch
⌒ **Ch:** chain(s)	
▬ **Sl st:** slip stitch(es)	**Tr:** treble(s)

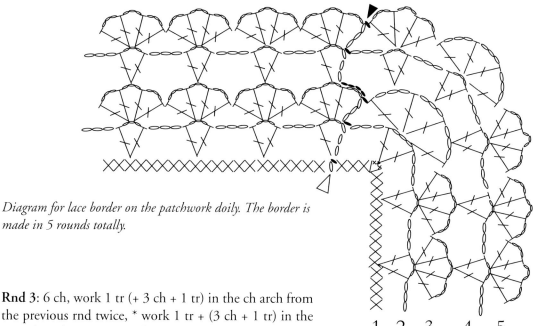

Diagram for lace border on the patchwork doily. The border is made in 5 rounds totally.

Rnd 3: 6 ch, work 1 tr (+ 3 ch + 1 tr) in the ch arch from the previous rnd twice, * work 1 tr + (3 ch + 1 tr) in the next ch arch 3 times, rep from *. Finish the rnd with 1 sl st in the 3rd ch from the beg of the rnd.

Rnd 4: Work 4 sl st over 4 st, 6 ch, work 1 tr, 3 ch in the next ch arch, miss 2 ch arches, work 1 tr + 3 ch + 1 tr in the next ch arch, continue like this.

Please notice that you have to work the following in each corner ch arch: 1 tr + 3 ch + 1 tr + 3 ch, finish the rnd

1   2   3   4   5

Tips

You can make some incredibly beautiful place mats with this fine and light lace border. Or napkin rings where the ring is made out of the linen fabric with lace borders on both sides. You just have to remember that the pattern must be divisible by 6.

With 1 sl st in the 3rd ch from the beg of the round.

Rnd 5: Worked like rnd 3 over all of the 112 grs.

Break the thread and start at a new square.

You only start the joining once the edge on the 2nd is almost finished. Meaning from the 5th rnd. Place the 2 squares facing each other with the front side upwards. See joining diagram as well. The 2nd ch between the 2nd and 3rd tr is replaced with 1 sl st, continue joining the 2 squares.

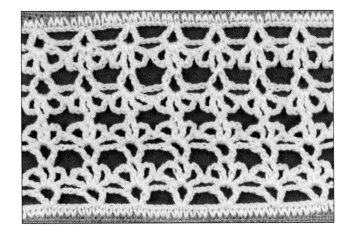

Detail photo of joining 2 edges. Please notice that the joining is almost invisible. The white lace makes a pretty contrast to the linen fabric.

Diagram for the edges of the doily and the joining technique. Start by working the edge from the starting arrow. Then finish the 2nd square, then the 3rd and at last the 4th square. The round motif (5) is worked separately and is not joined to the 4 middle chain arches until the last round.

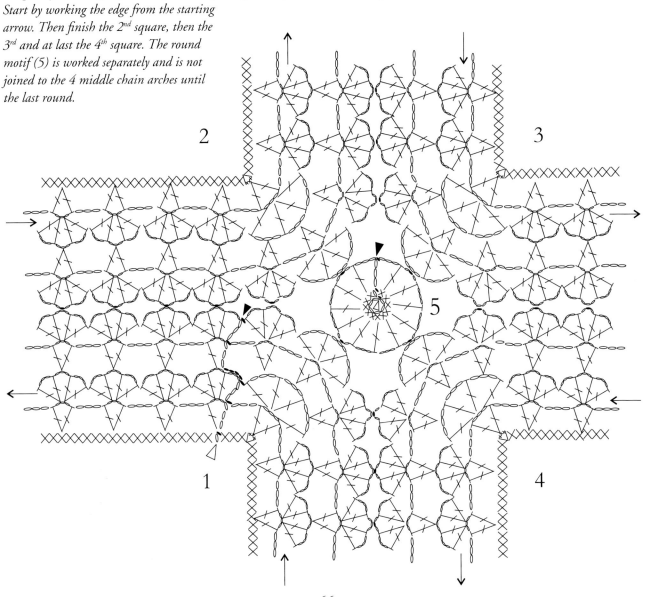

The 3rd and 4th square is joined in the same way.

At last work the round motifs, which are joined together with the squares in the middle hole that appears when the squares are joined.

Round motif

Make 6 ch, form a ring with 1 sl st in the 1st ch.

Follow diagram 5.

Detail photo. Here you can see the middle motif, where the round motif is joined at the chain stitches of the 4 corners.

Tips – finding the right way to mount a work

There are many ways to mount a work and you have to consider which way of mounting a work will look the best each time.

When joining the parts you obtain a completely flat seam, which also is partially elastic. You could also sew the work together by hand or on a sewing machine. Both ways require some care.

Tips – mounting on a sewing machine

You can quite easily mount you crochet work on a sewing machine, but this requires some accuracy.

1. Always make a sewing test of the seam you want to use.
2. Dampen the edges so they are completely flat.
3. Pin and tack the pieces together before sewing them together on the machine.
4. Dampen the seams and the rest of the work carefully after the sewing.

Antique doily

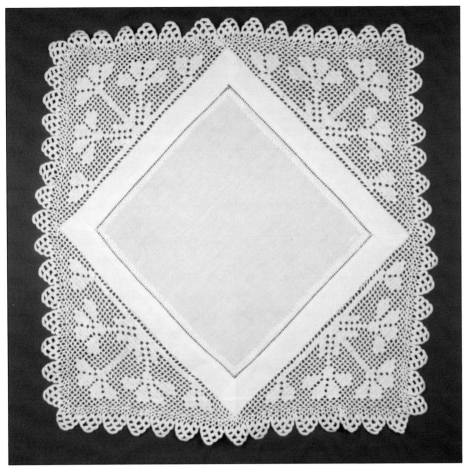

Doily with filet crochet corners. Measures 33 x 33 cm. Privately owned.
I found this lovely little doily in an antique shop in England 15 years ago. It is worked on very fine cotton fabric with hook no. 0.60 or 0.75. The corners are worked onto the fabric separately.

Dimensions: 39 x 39 cm.

Materials: white Cordonnet Special no. 20 from DMC. Running length is approx 160 m/20 g. Crochet hook no. 1.00. Suitable fabric would be bleached linen with 12 threads per cm.

Tension: 20 meshes/24 rows = 10 cm. It is very important to work a test first that is about 20 x 20 meshes to figure out how large a piece of fabric you have to cut for a total of 59 meshes = the width of the fabric + 2 cm for seam. Please notice that the parenthesis is repeated the amount of times stated immediately afterwards.

Preparing the fabric: Cut a 33 x 33 cm square. Zigzag the edges to prevent fraying. Fold in the edges reducing the measures to 29.5 x 29.5 cm cm, iron the edges sharp.

Corner

See diagram. Beg by working the first corner along the side making a total of 59 meshes.

Row 1: Beg like this – fasten the thread at the corner with 1 sl st. Follow the diagram.

Next corner
Fasten the thread at the top of the tr from row 1 in the 1st corner with 1 sl st, 4 ch + 1 tr at the same place as the tr (2 ch, miss 4 – 5 threads, 1 tr approx 3 – 4 threads below the edge) 59 times.
Follow the pattern in the diagram from row 2.

Continue until you have made all 4 corners.

Border

Work a narrow border with tr and ch around the doily in 2 rounds. See diagram for border.

Rnd 1: Fasten the thread in the 2nd mesh from the corner in the dtr with 1 sl st, + 6 ch + 1 tr, * work 1 tr + 3 ch + 1 tr in the next mesh, rep from *, finish the rnd with 1 sl st in the 3rd ch from the beg of the rnd + 2 sl st over 2 ch.

Rnd 2: 6 ch + 1 tr in the same arch, work 1 tr + 3 ch + tr in the next mesh, work 120 arches totally around the table cloth for the pointed border to add up. Finish the rnd with 1 sl st in the 3rd ch from the beg of the rnd.

Rnd 3: 1 ch, 6 dc over the 1st arch, (work 7 dc in the next arch) 119 times, finish the rnd with 1 sl st in the 1st ch of the rnd.

Points

Finally work the small points around the edges of the table cloth. Finish each point separately. See diagram for point.

Row 1: Fasten the thread in the arch at the corner with 1 sl st. Follow the diagram.

Break the thread, fasten off and start a new point in the 4th dc of the next arch.

Work 15 points along each side.

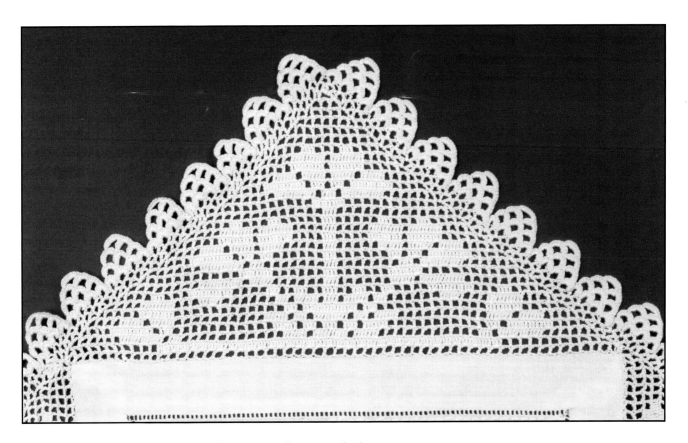

Detail photo of a crochet corner. Here the pattern is shown completely.
Around the table cloth a 3 round narrow edge is worked. The fine small points are each finished separately.

⊖	**Ch:** chain(s)
➖	**Sl st:** slip stitch(es)
×	**Dc:** double crochet(s)
⊺	**Tr:** treble(s)
⊼	**Dtr:** double treble(s)
▷	**Start:** Start here
▶	**End:** End here

Tips – starting a larger work.

If you have to make chains for a larger work like i.e. a table cloth or a curtain, is it very easy to miscount the chains while working them. Work a number of chains on a second thread in the same yarn as the rest of the work, which may be prolonged should it be needed. When the work reaches the required length, the remaining chains on the second thread may be unravelled.

Tips

It is easy to enlarge the signatures and thus making them even more clear by enlarging them on a photocopier.

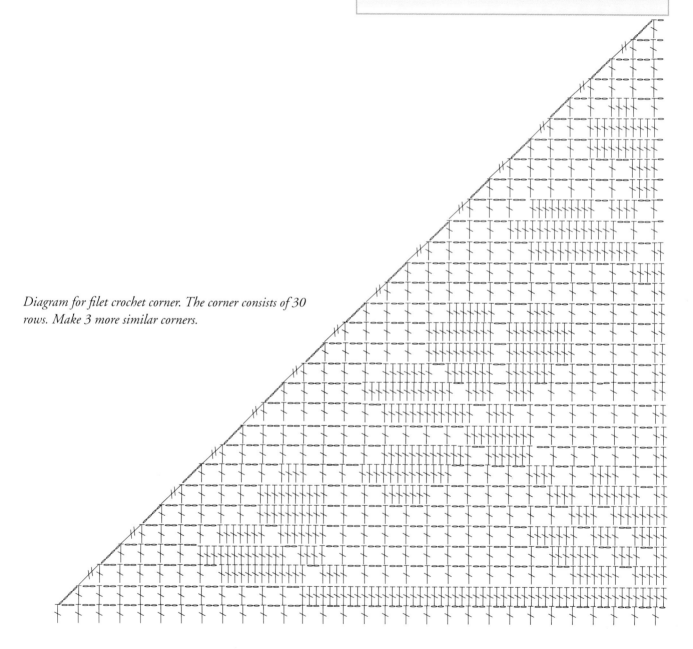

Diagram for filet crochet corner. The corner consists of 30 rows. Make 3 more similar corners.

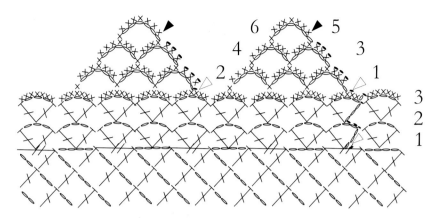

Diagram for border. The diagram shows the 3 first rounds on the border that is worked around the table cloth.

The points are each finished separately. Work 15 points along each side.

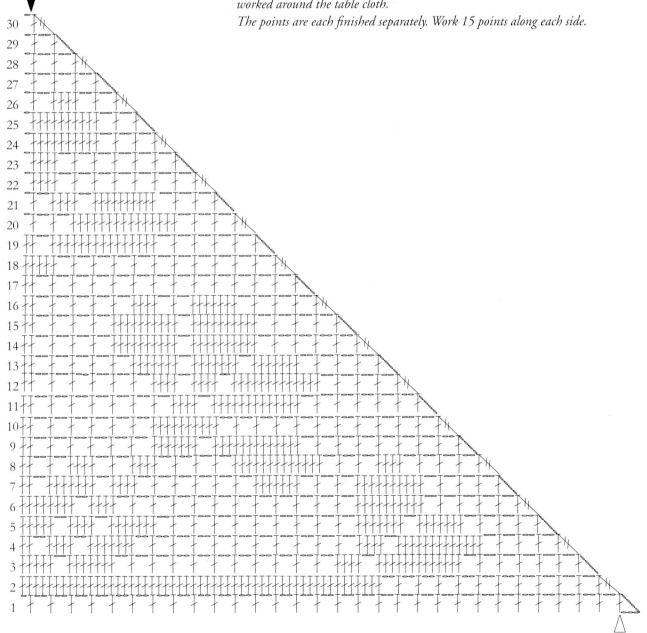

Square motif

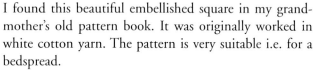

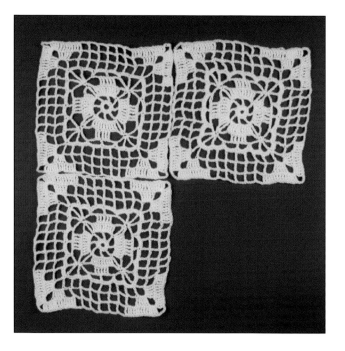

I found this beautiful embellished square in my grand-mother's old pattern book. It was originally worked in white cotton yarn. The pattern is very suitable i.e. for a bedspread.

Dimensions: 15 x 15 cm.

Materials: Approx 100 g white Petra no. 5 from DMC. Running length is approx 420 m/100 g. Crochet hook no. 1.50.

Square: Make 6 ch, form at ring with 1 sl st.
Follow the diagram.

Tips. How to make a 3, 4 or 5 double treble.
Yarn over the hook 3, 4 or 5 times, meaning the amount correlating to the chosen stitch. Insert the hook in the next stitch, yarn over the hook and pull one loop through the stitch, then work all the stitches on the hook in pairs.

Tips.
You can work approx 10 squares from 100 g Petra from DMC using hook no. 1.50.

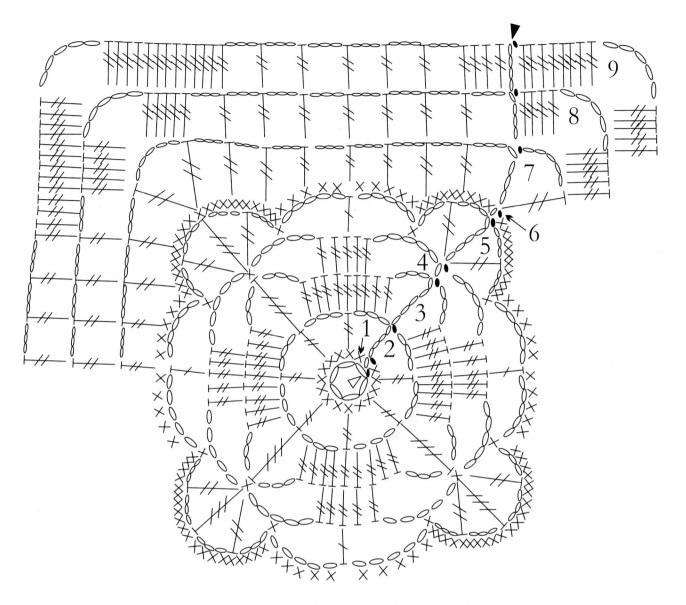

Diagram for square. The square is made in rounds. The 6 first rounds are shown completely. Round 7 – 9 are only shown partially.

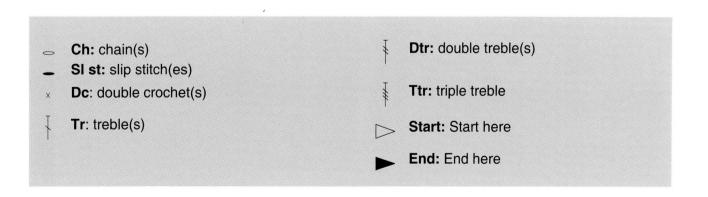

⊝	**Ch:** chain(s)	╫	**Dtr:** double treble(s)
▬	**Sl st:** slip stitch(es)		
×	**Dc:** double crochet(s)	╫	**Ttr:** triple treble
		▷	**Start:** Start here
┼	**Tr:** treble(s)	►	**End:** End here

Bedspread

This is a true classic, which is guaranteed to give you sweet dreams. It is a lovely needlework, which is quite easy to take along as it consists of a collection of hexagonal rosettes. The size of the bedspread depends on how many motifs you work.

Dimensions: approx 145(220) x 220 cm = single (double) bed.

Materials: approx 3000(4500) g ecru Petra Art 993A no. from DMC. Running length 420 m/100 g. Crochet hook no. 2. Work 60(94) complete motives + 6(10) half motives.

Tension: the first 4 rounds are 4.5 x 4.5 cm. 1 hexagon is approx 25 x 25 from tip to tip. It is very important to maintain the tension throughout the work. If the tension is not correct, you will have to use a finer or thicker hook.

The bedspread is made of hexagonal rosettes.

The buds

The buds in rounds 3 and 16 are worked like this: (yarn over the hook, insert the hook in the stitch, yarn over and pull the thread through the stitch…

… yarn over again and pull through 8 loops on the hook…

… until the loop is the same height as the rest of the stitch) 4 times…

… yarn over and pull through the last 2 loops on the hook = 1 bud.

Hexagonal rosette

Work 60(94) hexagonal motives totally.

Follow diagram 1.
Make 6 ch and form a ring with 1 sl st in the 1st ch.

Follow diagram 2. See page 76.
Rnd 9 and 10: See photo and text on the next page.

Please notice: Rnds 11 – 16 starts with 3 ch = not stated in the recipe. The parenthesis is rep the amount stated right after it.

Diagram 1. Shows the part with the rosette on the hexagonal motif for the bedspread. The diagram for the first 4 rounds is completely shown. The next 5 rounds are only partially shown. Work on according to diagram 2 on page 78. A + B indicate the stitches, where to insert the hook in on round 9.

4 chains

How to work round 9 and 10

Rnd 9: work 4 ch and miss 30 st from the hook, place the 2 corners front against front and insert the hook through both layers in both the 30th + 20th st…

… in stitch no. 25 + 15 from the hook, work 1 dc, stitch no. 24 + 16, 23 + 17, 22 + 18 and 21 + 19 = a total of 5 dc) 14 times.

… work 1 dc, continue working dc in stitch no. 29 + 21, 28 + 22, 27 + 23 and 26 + 24 = a total of 5 dc, (4 ch, insert the hook through both layers…

Rnd 10: work (5 dc over 5 dc, 4 dc over 4 ch) 16 times.

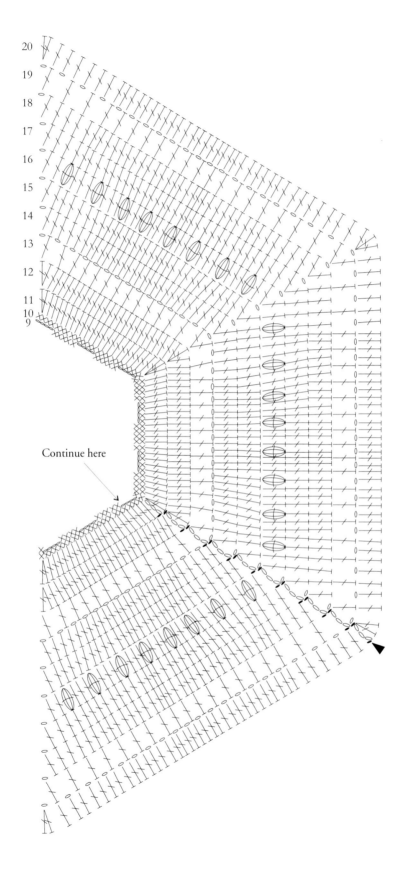

Continue here

20
19
18
17
16
15
14
13
12
11
10
9

Diagram 2. This is the second part of the diagram for hexagonal motif. It is worked in rounds.

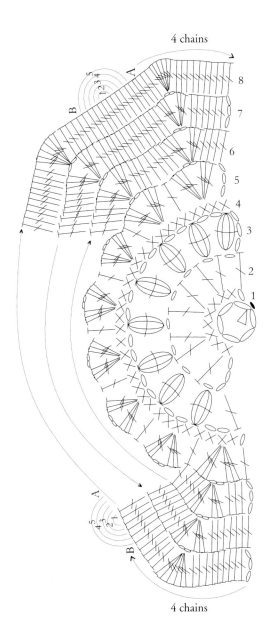

4 chains

4 chains

Diagram 3. This shows the part for a half motif. The first 5 rounds for the rosette are completely shown.

A half motif

Work 6(10) half motifs totally.
Follow diagram 3. Work 6 ch and form a ring with 1 sl st in the 1st ch.

Rnd 9: see also photo on page 77. Work 4 ch, miss 30 st from the hook, place 2 corners front against front, insert the hook through both layers, work 1 dc in both st no. 30 + 20, continue working dc in st no. 29 + 21, 28 + 22, 27 + 33 and 26 + 24 = 5 dc totally, (4 ch, insert the hook through both layers in st no. 25 + 15 from the hook and work 1 dc, the same in st no. 24 + 16, 23 + 17, 22 + 18 and 21 + 19 = 5 dc totally) 7 times.

Follow diagram 4.

Break the thread.

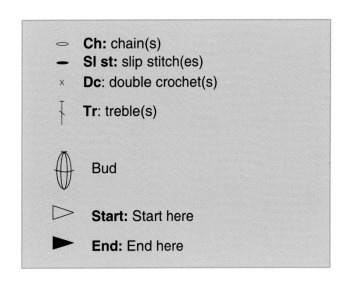

⬯	**Ch:**	chain(s)
▬	**Sl st:**	slip stitch(es)
×	**Dc:**	double crochet(s)
⊺	**Tr:**	treble(s)
⬮		Bud
▷	**Start:**	Start here
▶	**End:**	End here

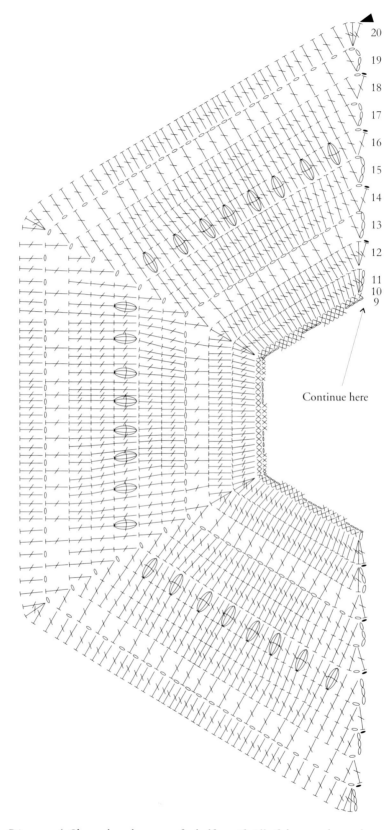

20
19
18
17
16
15
14
13
12
11
10
9

Continue here

Diagram 4. Shows the other part of a half motif. All of the rounds are shown completely.

80

Mounting

Stretch all of the motifs out with pins to the correct measurement before sewing them tog.
Iron them under a moist piece of fabric. Leave the motifs until they are completely dry.

Sew the motifs tog with whip stitches.

It is easiest to sew the motifs tog in long rows with 9 and 8 motifs respectively, and then sew the rows together at last.

Look at the chart how the rounds are placed in every 2nd round.

Working chart for bedspread for a single(double) bed. 145(220) x 220 cm. The chart shows how the bedspread is combined of 60(94) complete motifs and 6(10) half motifs.

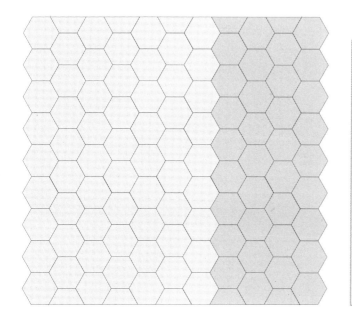

Tips on dyeing

When you start a large project, then make sure that the yarn has the same dye lot. This means that it originates from the same dye lot, which may be seen on the label around the yarn. Differences in colour will become very obvious when the work is sewn together.
So make sure that you buy enough yarn because it will take some time to make such a large crochet work.

Tips. Yarn consumption for the bedspread.

You use approx 45 g of Hermina from DMC for 1 hexagonal. If your bed does not have the same measurement as stated here, you can calculate the consumption of yarn. Remember also to include yarn for edges and mounting.

Edge of the bedspread

See diagram 5.

Rnd 1: Fasten the thread at the edge with 1 sl st, 3 ch, continue working 1 tr in every st. Follow the diagram.

Please notice that along the pointed edge it is necessary work 3 sts tog to dec at join of motifs + work 3 tr in the same st to inc at points, this applies for rnd 1 – 4. See detail photos as well. Finish the rnd 1 sl st in the 3rd ch from the beg of the rnd.

Break the thread and fasten all loose threads. Stretch the bedspread out with pins in the stated measurement and iron it carefully under a moist piece of fabric. Leave the work until it is completely dry.

Detail photo of the edge. Here the decreases of 3 stitches are shown. The decreases are placed over the same stitches in every round.

This detail photo shows how to make the increase of 3 stitches worked in the same corner stitch. This is necessary to obtain the pointed effect.

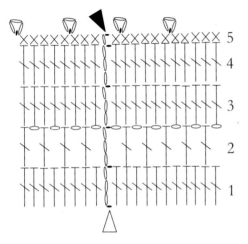

Diagram 5. Edge of the bedspread. The edge is made in 5 rounds.

The edge of holes around the bedspread surmounts the work beautifully. The final touch is the round with small picots that accentuates the nostalgic pattern.

Scarf made in knot stitches

This airy scarf worked in knot stitches is very soft and falls beautifully. Please notice the little pompom edge at the ends of the scarf.

Dimensions: approx 25 x 140 cm.

Materials: approx 100 g white Petra no. 5 from DMC. Running length approx 420 m/100 g. Crochet hook no. 1.50.

Follow the diagram.

Pattern

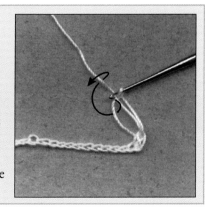

Row 1: work 1 dc in the 2nd ch from the hook * the loop on the hook is pulled until it is 1-2 cm long, yarn over and pull the thread through the loop…

…insert the hook through the loop, formed behind the long loop, yarn over again and pull the thread through, you now have 2 loops on the hook, yarn over and pull the thread through the 2 loops on the hook = 1 dc.

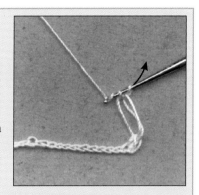

Now you have made the first knot. Rep from * one more time then you have made 2 knots.

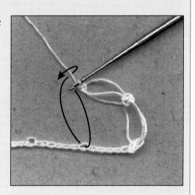

Miss 5 ch on the starting chain and work 1 dc in the 6th ch. Rep from * = 10 knots at the end of the row.

Row 2 and every following row: Turn the work with 3 knots…

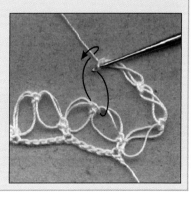

... then work * 1 dc around the 1st long loop from the previous row, where you work around the 2 loops + 1 dc around the next long loop, again only around the 2 loops...

...then work 2 knots. Rep from *.
Row 2 makes the pattern and is repeated. Turn every row with 3 knots.

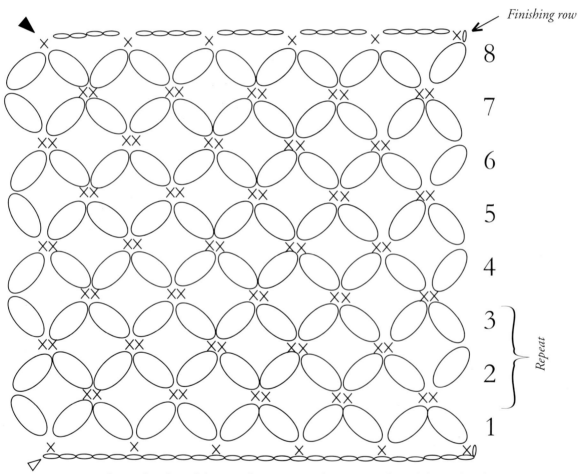

Finishing row

8
7
6
5
4
3
2
1

Repeat

Diagram 1. Pattern for scarf made with knot stitches. Row 2 and 3 is repeated until the work is the required length. At last you work a finishing row as shown in the diagram.

⊖ **Ch:** chain(s)

× **Dc:** double crochet(s)

◯ Long loop

▷ **Start:** start here

► **End:** end here

Double crochet edge with pompoms

Row 1: Fasten the thread in the 1st dc with 1 sl st, work 6 dc over every ch arch, work 1 dc in the knot.

Row 2 – 3: 1 ch replacing the 1st dc on the row, work dc over all of the st.

Row 4: See how to do this in the photo and follow the diagram.

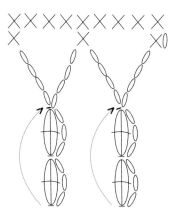

Diagram 2. Pompom edge for scarf worked with knot stitches. The arrow shows the place where you insert the hook and work a slip stitch, when 2 half pompons are joined.

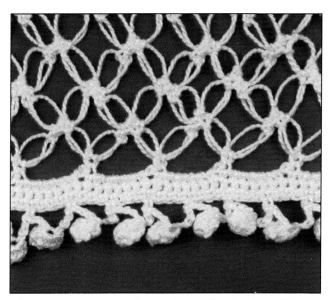

The pompom edge gives the scarf a very fine finishing. The edge is very easy to make.

Pompom edge

Row 4: 1 ch = 1st dc * 7 ch (work 3 unfinished tr in the 3rd ch from the hook = 4 loops on the hook, yarn over and pull the thread through all 4 loops at once)…

… 3 ch, rep from *. Join 2 half pompoms and work 1 sl st in the 4th ch from the beg…

… work 4 ch, miss 3 dc at the edge, 1 dc in the next ch, rep from * - *. This makes a total of 18 pompoms. Turn the work and work another similar edge.

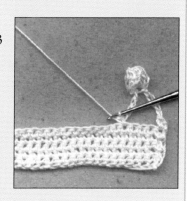

- ⬯ **Ch:** chain(s)
- — **Sl st:** slip stitch(es)
- × **Dc:** double crochet(s)
- ⬯ **3 tr cl:** 3 treble cluster worked in the same stitch.

Assisi style crochet

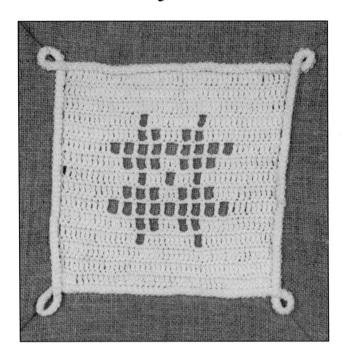

Here I have made an Assisi style star motif and mounted it on a pillow so you may glimpse the fabric through the crochet. Finally, a crochet trimming surrounds the motif itself. This technique is called Assisi style crochet.

Dimensions: 10 x 10 cm. The pillow, which the square is mounted on, measures 30 x 30 cm.

Materials: approx 50 g white Babylo no. 20/12 from DMC. Running length approx 400 m/50 g. Crochet hook no. 1.25.

Tension: 1 square measures 10 x 10 cm. It is very important to maintain the tension throughout the work in order to obtain a satisfying end result. If the tension does not fit, you will have to use a finer or thicker hook. Please notice that the parenthesis is repeated as many times as it is stated right after it.

Assisi style square
Make 54 ch. Follow the diagram.

Crochet trimming
Work a string at approx 50 cm.

See how the string is made at page 32.

Mounting
Sew the motif onto the middle of the pillow. Sew the trimming around the edges of the motif with small invisible stitches.

Tips. Raised treble crochet
Work a ring of chains, yarn over the hook once and insert the hook in the 4th stitch from the hook. Yarn over and pull the thread through, yarn over and pull through the 1st loop on the hook, yarn over and pull through 2 loops, yarn over and pull through the remaining 2 loops = 1 raised treble. The raised treble is a bit shorter then the double treble but much more beautiful to look at and is especially suitable for working rounds. The star motif in Assisi style crochet may also be worked in raised trebles.

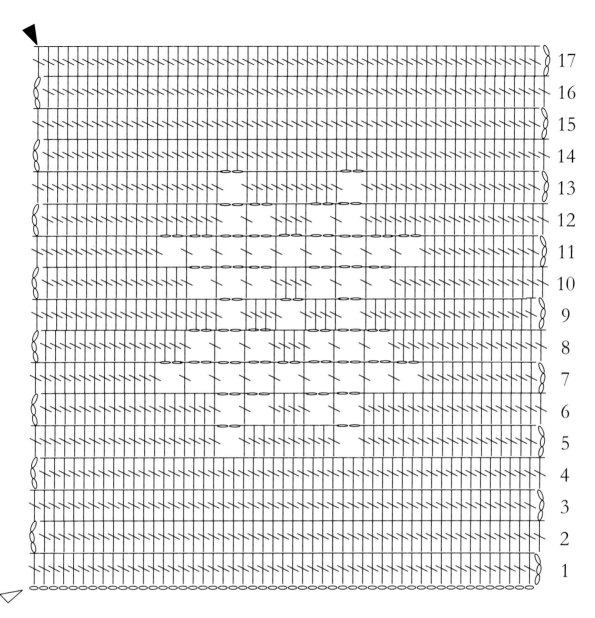

Diagram for star motif in Assisi style crochet. Begin at the starting arrow. Make 54 chains. The square is made in 17 rows.

Tips

Assisi style crochet is another name for reversed filet crochet where the motif itself appears voided. This means that where you would expect an open background in ordinary filet crochet, in Assisi style crochet it is filled with trebles. The pattern itself appears in an open pattern – this gives a new and exciting effect.

⊖ **Ch:** chain(s)

⌇ **Tr:** treble(s)

▷ **Start:** Start here

► **End:** End here

Index